SILICON TRENCHES

Dial-Up to AI, Building It as We Fly It

By

Mike Choate, PE

CONTENTS

PRAISE FOR	v
Preface	xi

PART ONE
MY JOURNEY THROUGH IT

Introduction	3
1. Where's The Hotline, Susie?	7
2. Keep an Open Mind	25
3. Change on the Horizon	39
4. Form, Fit, and Function	47
5. When Are You Going to Get the Damned Thing Fixed?	61
6. Who's The Boss?	71
7. The Database Monster	89
8. It Shouldn't Fail Like That!	95
9. Garbage In, Garbage Out	111

PART TWO
A GUIDE TO INNOVATIVE DESIGN

10. Innovative Training Elements for Solution Engineering Teams	119
11. Innovative Tools for Post-Silicon Solution Engineering	131
12. Staffing for Solutions Engineering	151
13. Communications	165
14. Conference Planning	179
Epilogue	189
Acknowledgments	201

Copyright © 2024 by Solutions Press, a subsidiary of Fairview Investments LLC, a Texas limited liability corporation.

All rights reserved. This book or any portion thereof may not be reproduced or used in any manner whatsoever without the express written permission of the publisher except for the use of brief quotations in a book review.

Printed in the United States of America

First Printing, 2024

ISBN _____

PRAISE FOR
MIKE CHOATE, P.E. AND "SILICON TRENCHES: DIAL-UP TO AI, BUILDING IT AS WE FLY IT"

"Mike has certainly been-there-done-that. We did the Field Service Bulletins which utilized your cause and effect approach: Determine the root cause is the best approach."

— ALBERT JOHNSON P.E.

"Mike Choate addresses the period of the computer industry that built the foundation for today's electronic, computerized world, the time when the computer industry was young when companies big and tiny were integrating their world with computers. Mike takes us up to the edge of the industry today, to the edge of the use of artificial intelligence. He talks about both inside the computer companies and inside the companies that adopted this technology. This book is both informative and educational. Enjoy."

— KATIE BARRETT, PENN STATE

OUTSTANDING ENGINEERING ALUMNI,
COMPUTER SCIENCE 1968

"Mike Choate is someone you would like on deck when the nuts come off the wheels as you try to launch a product."

— JERRY ZURASKI, MICROPROCESSOR ARCHITECT

"I only have fond memories of working with [Mike] and each of [his] team members during the early days at AMD. Staying up for several day stretches, discovering all the land minds together, and overcoming every obstacle one at a time. It was like being back on the battlefield of Desert Storm for me, and I perversely miss them some days. "

— GARY ASHMORE, MBA, MPA, GM, LOWER TRINITY GCD

ABBREVIATIONS

The following list is a compilation of abbreviations and acronyms used in the book.

Abbreviation	Meaning
AI	artificial intelligence
ASIC	application-specific integrated circuit
BIOS	basic input/output system
BLWP	branch and load workspace pointer
BM	bus master
BOM	bill of materials
BPI	bits per inch
BT	British Telecom
COBOL	common business-oriented language
CPU	central processing unit
DEC	Digital Equipment Corporation
DNOS	Distributed Networking Operating System
ECO	engineering change order
EOS	electrical overstress
ESD	electrical static discharge

ABBREVIATIONS

Abbreviation	Meaning
ESD	electrical static discharge
FPGA	field programmable gate array
IC	integrated circuit
JTAG	joint test action group
Kb	kilobit
KB	kilobyte
NAK or NACK	negative acknowledgement
OEM	original equipment manufacturer
PC	personal computer
PE	phase-encoded / professional engineer
PFM	pure f-ing magic
PROM	programmable read-only memory
PWB	printed wiring board
QA	quality assurance
QAM	quadrature amplitude modulation
RAM	random access memory
SSO	simultaneous switching output
SSSD	single-sided single-density
SUT	System Under Test
VAR	value added reseller

PREFACE

As a newly appointed young manager of a hardware and software testing group in Silicon Hills, I was keenly aware of the complexities and responsibilities of my new role. The task at hand was daunting: I needed to inform senior executives and individual engineers about the failures of our latest designs during the research and development of the company. Oftentimes, the designs did not pass our rigorous tests, and this news could cause the company to have to delay product launches and shipments.

Seeking guidance, I turned to Mike Choate, a seasoned professional known for his expertise and practical wisdom in our company. He dealt very often with all levels of management and customers in delivering good and bad data as a senior debugging expert.

I approached Mike with a mix of apprehension and anticipation, eager to learn the secret of Mike's always-positive working relationship with others in spite of the bad news he sometimes had to deliver when finding and researching the root cause of a failure. His demeanor was calm and encouraging as he listened to my concerns. I explained the dual challenge: communicating the design failure to senior executives, who were often impatient and demanding, and to the engineers, whose hard work and creativity were tied up in these designs.

Mike began by emphasizing the importance of being direct and respectful. "Gary," he said, "the key to delivering bad news is honesty tempered with empathy. Always start with the facts. Be transparent about the issues and back up your statements with solid data. This approach shows that your conclusions are based on thorough research and not just opinion or personal attacks."

He stressed the necessity of having all relevant data at hand. "When you present the failure to the executives, bring all the test results, error logs, and any other documentation that supports your findings. This will help you make a compelling case and demonstrate that your team has left no stone unturned in their analysis. It's important to show that the failure isn't due to negligence or lack of effort, but rather a part of the development process."

Mike also shared insights on maintaining a positive relationship with the engineers. "Approach the engineers with respect for their work. Acknowledge the effort they put into the design and the innovative ideas they contributed. Explain the specific points of failure and discuss potential solutions. This way, they feel involved in the process and see it as a learning opportunity rather than a personal failure."

One of the most valuable pieces of advice Mike gave me was about the timing and setting of these conversations. "Choose a time and place where you can have a focused, uninterrupted discussion. Avoid delivering bad news in a rushed or public setting, like in a conference call with dozens of attendees. This shows that you value their time and contributions." I learned to give key individuals a heads-up before presenting the information company-wide, allowing them time to internalize the information, be prepared to address it, and develop the next steps to correct it.

Additionally, over our working relationship, Mike often

suggested a few other strategies to handle such situations more effectively:

1. Building Trust: "Establish a rapport with both executives and engineers well before any issues arise. Regular updates and open communication channels build a foundation of trust, making it easier to handle crises. 'Positive Framing': Whenever possible, frame the conversation in a way that focuses on solutions rather than just the problems. Highlight what can be learned from the failure and how it can lead to better outcomes in the future."
2. Following Up: "After the initial discussion, follow up with both the executives and engineers. Provide updates on the steps being taken to address the issues and any progress made. This continuous engagement shows that you are proactive and committed to resolving the problems."
3. Encouraging Feedback: "Encourage engineers to share their thoughts and suggestions. This not only helps in finding better solutions but also empowers them and makes them feel valued." Mike's advice was instrumental in helping me navigate these challenging conversations. By being direct, respectful, and prepared, I was able to maintain positive relationships with both the senior executives and the engineers not only in the United States but also worldwide. These tools served me well when working with others in parts of our company. Over time, this approach fostered a culture of trust and collaboration, ultimately benefiting our projects, my teams, and the company as a whole.

In retrospect, that first conversation with Mike was a turning point in my managerial journey. It equipped me with the tools to handle difficult situations with grace and effectiveness, a lesson I carry with me to this day and have tried to convey to those I manage as well.

Thanks to Mike's guidance, I learned to personally handle difficult conversations with both respect and clarity, building trust and strengthening the confidence of my team, executives, and design engineers from around the globe in the R&D process.

Silicon Trenches reads nicely and should inspire those who are open to learning new things from a truly professional and intelligent person like you.

- Gary

PART ONE
MY JOURNEY THROUGH IT

INTRODUCTION

What exactly goes on behind the scenes at the heart of computer development and the help desk?

If you're a help desk professional, have you ever wondered why procedures are the way they are? Do you wonder why so many callers are angry? Do you feel any pressure to perform your job error-free? Worse yet, do you feel powerless to change the help desk process?

If you're on the other side of the phone, are you one of the millions of people who hate to call any help desk? Do you hate "holding for the next available support professional"? Do you find yourself begging to be expedited to the absolute best phone assistance possible? Don't you just want to let the people on the other end of the line know that, if everyone received quality service, it would eliminate that horrendous dial-and-hold crisis facing help desk professionals and callers today?

Yes, there's new tech to help you better navigate through some of the more mundane points of contact between computers and callers, but even AI help desks are limited to the information they can access and analyze. Even with the new-and-improved methods, sometimes it's still a no-help desk.

But I've been there.

THE "WHY"

This book has been a long time coming. It's taken me years to get everything down on paper, but it's time these stories are told.

I've been a helpdesk agent, a customer, a computing student, and a new engineering hire. You might say I've seen it all. My many years of experience have resulted in some great friends and many of them have prompted me to write this book.

If you're reading this book, it means you have questions of your own.

Part I of this book is a collection of stories about my journey through the dark trenches of product development and technical support in Silicon Hills, Silicon Valley, and beyond in the early pre-artificial Intelligence computing days. Read it as both a memoir and a guide for people who are going through their own struggles with misbehaving technology. There is always a solution, even if it's difficult to find. Part II is a handbook for building trust in volatile product development and technical support environments.

This book tells the story of the first 25 years of my career, primarily living in the world of escalation to level 3 tech support and the challenges I faced. This by no means reduces the importance of the everyday help desk persons who answer calls, follow the scripts, and help thousands of callers. I am just one of hundreds of engineers who are called upon by companies to analyze problems that cannot be normally answered by the help desk. By telling these stories, I hope to give the reader an insight into what goes on behind the scenes of major product development as we all strive to make this world a better place.

From this book Part I, you'll learn:

- The highs and lows of help desks on both sides of the phone
- Lessons of the past from problem-solving stories that require patience, persistence, and perseverance.

In Part II, you will learn Advice for innovative planning, design, staffing, running meetings, and team management.

CHAPTER ONE

WHERE'S THE HOTLINE, SUSIE?

WHEN I FIRST STARTED WORK AS A HELP DESK professional in Jan 1979, we answered all customer phone calls personally. We started with an overhead ringer, but it was eventually replaced with a loud buzzer when the phone rang. When the buzzer sounded, we picked up the phone handset and pressed **3 on the keypad to transfer the incoming group call to our workstation. We were the experts. No phone menus and no call screeners. We worked on one call and one customer at a time until the customer was satisfied or stopped asking questions. The phone number to reach our help desk was not a toll-free number. Callers paid for long-distance charges.

My employer, a US firm that went by its initials, was an Original Equipment Manufacturer (OEM) for the global enterprise mini-computer market. We designed, manufactured, and marketed 16-bit mini-computer hardware and our own proprietary multi-tasking operating system software to distributors and vertical systems integrators (a.k.a. Value Added Reseller or VARs). This was before PCs came to the scene with the 8-bit 8086 processor in 1981.

While a high-school intern, Daren A., a literal genius,

invented the interface protocol to access a 20-bit memory system address while working on our prior generation computers limited to a 16-bit address. This multiplied the amount of system memory the CPU could access by sixteen, from 64KB to 1MB.

MS-DOS was a single-threaded OS. That means only one program, task, or process could "run" at a time. In contrast, our software divided the available time into slices of a few milliseconds allowing active "tasks" to execute for a rotating prioritized slice of time each minute, so every minute, dozens of "task programs" could progress and give the appearance that all the programs were running at the same time. Higher priority tasks got the most time slices. The computer was the central nerve of the system, and there were many remote terminals connected for data entry and/or data collection. Some systems had up to 256 connected terminals. Unlike many early PC-like computers, our computer used distributed microprocessor-based state machines to perform Input/Output to mass storage, network, printers, and terminals leaving the Central processor to concentrate on compute functions.

The VARs packaged them with custom software and/or hardware for the end users. Many of our computers were installed at transportation-related sales and service centers, including car rentals, farm implements, and airlines. We often received calls from developers and scientists who used our computers. Some of my favorite calls were from Los Alamos National Laboratory.

My manager's name was Susie B. She had a Ph.D. in Physics and knew how to manage engineers—she got out of our way and let us do our job. She hated micro-managing as much as we did. If we needed something to do our job, she made it her highest priority. Everyone called us the "hotline," and everyone knew Susie was in charge. The firm's management ranks were male-dominated at the time. Susie was the only female manager, and she would not tolerate being ignored or being treated differently than male managers. If upper management started whining about her budget, she would threaten to shut down the hotline for just one day. If no one answers the phone, angry customers make a big fuss to HQ, and Susie gets an emergency pager call asking, "Where is the Hotline?" The first time would be the last time it would ever be shut down.

Wow, can you imagine how nice it would be to speak to a live person when you call a help desk today?

We rarely had free time between calls, but when we did, we tried to take advantage of it. We couldn't take breaks as a group like other factory workers because someone had to answer the phones during business hours, 8 am to 5 pm. When we could, we would exchange data on the problems we solved.

I learned that not all experts are created equal and not all callers with the same problem described it the same way. Not even close. There was no consistent approach to finding a fix. Everyone had their own techniques and experiences, and they always worked to find the perfect solution. Each expert had different techniques for getting the same information, and they often took different approaches to finding an answer or fix. By exchanging information between ourselves, we could change our personal techniques to find the best for each situation.

We wanted to make the help desk as helpful as possible, so I took the role of mentor. Eventually, management saw the need to implement a consistent approach to responding to incoming calls from a mixture of user types and locations.

THE NATURAL APPROACH

I was lucky and got called to work on the help desk at just the right time in help desk evolution and in my career.

As I worked on different teams later in my career, I applied this brainstorming technique very successfully. If everything works right, natural work groups have a native instinct to learn and improve through synergistic teamwork if compensation and bonuses are based on both team and individual effort. This way, if everyone appreciates the shared knowledge gained by helping someone, then you're motivated to contribute to the team. But, if you sit on the knowledge, only the person you help benefits, and your teammates have little incentive to help you in the future.

Some organizations are so self-centered and myopic that they don't see the benefit of a free exchange of information. In many organizations, the working environment is "cut-throat." People have been watching too much reality TV if you ask me. This isn't "Survivor." It should be about helping the customer and about building a successful team.

In the early days, we didn't have the Internet, e-mail, and the World Wide Web. We had the "Internet," but it consisted of a 1200 baud dial-up service to universities to do text-based research, or to find online catalogs of books and articles[1]. We used electronic bulletin boards more often than the Internet. Computer magazines of the day had listings of electronic bulletin board phone numbers, and very few were toll-free.

Dial-up used normal phone lines connected to MODEM (Modulator/Demodulator) and would negotiate or perform the connection handshake with a computer MODEM at the other end. The computer MODEM had a speaker to allow the handshake sequence of *beeps, boops, squawks, screeches,* and buzzing noises to be heard if a human did not answer. Early dial-up machines had a handset receptacle. The landline-wired phone handset would be plugged into the receptacle and the connection speed was limited. Eventually, MODEMs improved to use digital high-speed data connections.

In those days, it was all about the help desk expert, specialist, technician, or engineer. He or she was a highly skilled person, usually an engineer with years of experience who understood how

---

1. Using the Internet could save library research time because you could access research documents electronically, albeit at a very, very slow data rate.

everything worked for at least one or more functional sub-products. If he or she didn't know how it worked, he or she knew whom to contact to get the best answer. Sometimes, the help desk was an intermediate career stop for designers between design projects. It was also a fantastic training opportunity for field engineers to work in the factory for a few days during training classes to see how the factory processes interacted with the field. It was a great cross-training opportunity for help-desk experts, too; we could work in a field sales office for two weeks annually to get to know the field people and meet customers face-to-face. The insight was always useful, and Susie required each of us to write comprehensive trip reports explaining what we learned and list recommendations for improvements.

Actually, the idea for a help desk group came from the realization that names and phone numbers of knowledgeable key employees in the factory were given out to field sales offices (FSO) because the FSO had questions and needed quick answers to help close a sale. Unfortunately, there were so many questions requiring valuable research time that key factory employees couldn't get their work done on schedule. So, we organized a new group to host a central place where sales engineers and end users could get help. We ultimately created sales engineer positions to support the FSOs. And the hotline was the go-to place to help the sales engineers.

Susie said I should also keep a bag packed in case of an emergency that required travel. I thought she was joking. I started working in the factory right out of college, and after only 3 years, I knew almost everything about how our computers worked at the design level. Because I understood how it worked, I could figure out how to fix almost anything. Soon after I arrived, our help desk team reorganized into sub-teams specializing in either hardware or software issues. Most of the calls were software calls, but sometimes, you needed a specialist who understood both hardware and software to make a judgment on the real root cause of the problem. That was me. I eventually became the internal one-man escalation team and would *average* completing 40 calls per day in a nine-hour day, including calls carried over from the previous day(s). Most folks only averaged eight to twelve completed calls. I may not have had the most experience, but my personality and ability to memorize details made my services indispensable.

Although I didn't specialize in software, I learned how to solve most software problems as I worked on hardware problems. I became more and more proficient at analyzing software problems and became known as the go-to person for solving any problem. Within a short time, I had memorized almost every telephone area code for every major city in the US and many common eleven-digit numbers for parts and assemblies used in our computer system.

Finding a Solution

Today, there are so many rules to make a call easier. The scripts they feed to employees today are broken into easy-to-read sections with clear directions. But, back when I started at the help desk, there was a lot more freedom to try new things.

Throughout my years at the help desk, I learned some key tricks to aid anyone going through the help desk themselves.

Memorizing Between the Lines

I can't nail down my exact memorization techniques, but there are three routines I used to memorize fine details. The human brain's memory cells function as a rapid associative pattern or image storage and recall system. Therefore, the steps I use to memorize are:

1. Mentally capture a picture of the word, number, experience, or sound and practice recalling the memory several times.
2. Silently think of a label/phrase for the memory and visualize placing the label in the memory.
3. Silently focus on saving the memory label/phrase for recall later by assigning a mental priority to the memory and reflecting on future situations where the recall of the memory is valuable. Think about setting a mental alarm clock to ring when you need to recall it, triggering the situation you predicted by recalling the memory.

Though these have been the most helpful to me, everyone has to develop their own strategies. There isn't a set-in-stone method to help aid your memorization, and I encourage anyone to find something that works best for them.

The Caller Scan

I FOUND IT WAS USEFUL TO SURVEY THE CALLER'S knowledge and experience quickly and then classify caller types into four knowledge-level categories:

1. Complete novice: No technical knowledge at all.
2. Some experience: Operator level who understands terms and can identify units.
3. Experienced: Well-versed in techno jargon and makes good suggestions.
4. Know-it-all egotist: Can't tell him anything because he already "knows it."

I enjoyed working with the complete novice and people with

some experience the most because they were usually good listeners and could follow instructions well. You could ask them questions with yes or no answers and get only the "yes" or "no" back, not some other unrelated explanation or question. You could tell them to do steps 1, 2, 3, and 4 in order, and they did it.

This was an especially hazardous zone with the know-it-all egotist.

The know-it-all was usually two or three steps ahead of you, doing things in the wrong order or something wrong altogether. You not only had to realize what they were doing but would have to reverse any changes they made and do it all over again, sometimes three or four times, to get it right. Many times, they were reluctant to tell you what they had already done. They often argued with me over what the data showed. I suspect it was a game to them, that they were trying to test us or make us squirm. I can see the thrill in that. I admit I like to ask questions I already know the answer to so that I make the other person squirm or feel uncomfortable. If you get someone off-balance, it's easier to force them to change their position.

The experienced folks were much better than the know-it-all type, but often took more time because they rushed and made mistakes along the way. They were also curious about how things worked, so I often had to slow down and explain why I did each step.

Looking for Trouble

THE HELP DESK OFTEN FACES CHALLENGES IN ITS ability to directly see failures and limitations in guiding customers through troubleshooting steps because they can't actually see what the problem is. If you've worked at the help desk, you've probably seen your fair share of these calls. How do you know how to solve a problem, especially if it's a difficult caller?

The basic process behind a successful trouble call involves:

1. Starting by listing the exact system configuration, including versions of hardware, software, firmware, and patches.
2. Defining the failure symptoms as completely as possible, including when the problem started and what changed before the first symptom.
3. Collecting and analyzing detailed failure data.
4. Determining possible cause(s) of failure.
5. Defining experiments to rule out or prove each possible cause.
6. Defining possible remedial and/or corrective actions.
7. Implementing possible fixes in order of least cost or time, whichever is most important.
8. Verifying and ensuring no additional hidden problems occur.
9. Fixed? If not yet, escalating up the technical chain or the managerial chain for additional assistance; if permitted, repeat steps 2-7 until it is fixed or until it goes away.
10. If applicable, brainstorming preventative actions with design and quality control teams.

I personally hated when a problem just went away without knowing what fixed it or why it worked. Eventually, it would come back to bite me. I recommend customer service departments have a database to track their non-reproducible failures and/or no-fault-found analysis tickets. Eventually, this data can be useful when the problem comes back.

I think this applies to most complex products. Take automobiles for example. Analyzing vehicle crashes could identify trends in product weakness that need redesigning for safety, assuming the cost of implementing such design changes doesn't kill product affordability. But what is it worth to save a life? People can't put a price on human life[2].

Obviously, if a computer hardware component is defective, the help desk can't repair that over the phone, but we can help isolate the failure to the lowest field replaceable component and tell the customer what to order or place a field service trouble call for a service engineer, requesting travel to the site so they can repair the system. The system field replaceable components were usually very large and expensive and not easily repaired by the customer without highly specified training[3]. Occasionally, we installed systems at highly secure locations and only people with security clearance could enter.

The help desk had an immense disadvantage because we couldn't see the failure directly. We could only see it through the eyes of the person on the other end of the phone. We had to know exactly what we wanted to see and communicate to the caller how to get to that information. This included asking the customer to read system messages, try running system commands, and/or dump or display error logs.

There is an important point here. This relates, in part, back to the ESO problem regarding the help desk people who were unable to help because the problem reported wasn't on their list of customer problems. It was misinterpreted as a problem that *was* on the list and the answer made sense for the interpreted question and problem, but not my problem. For the help desk to know what types of data are useful in determining the cause or source of failure, he or she must be familiar with every type of data in the

---

2. More people had a life-changing injury than were killed and implementing seat belts, therefore, seat belts became mandatory. I remember when new cars cost about $2,000 and seat belts were optional equipment. I learned to drive in a car that had no seatbelts. I remember taking cross-country drives with my family as a young child without a child car seat or seat belts.
3. Occasionally, we installed systems at highly secure locations and only people with security clearance could enter.

system, especially architectural knowledge. In my case, I had calculated a value for unused money based on debits and credits, and their system had no label or name for it. With no label, it couldn't be found in a database search. This is a big difference from today's help desk to the early help desk.

Today, the help desk usually works with flow charts and help desk troubleshooting software that guides them through the most common fault isolation techniques. If the data indicates something that is not on the guide or chart, the automated tools usually can't assist the help desk in discovering it. So, either the help desk tries to make sense of what you told them, or they make it up to get you to go away. The help desk's primary motivation is to complete the call ticket. They are often rated on how many calls they complete. Only a highly experienced help desk individual can recognize an exception to the norm and either risk punishment by deviating from the standard procedure or escalate it to their management.

There is another danger of updating the troubleshooting scripts with incorrect call data collection information. In a large call center, no one may realize the scripts are directing resolution steps using invalid historical call completion records if it finds a trend in the data that wasn't true to begin with.

As a help desk pro, I recommend taking the following actions for call problem match exceptions.

1. Repeat what you heard the caller say to ensure you understand the problem statement.
2. Tell the caller that their symptom is an exception to the normal procedure so the caller knows what to expect.
3. If possible, follow established procedures for call exceptions such as escalating to senior help desk personnel.

4. If supported by policy, begin investigating the caller's problem in more detail to escalate to the next level more successfully, but don't fabricate solutions out of thin air or make the user do steps that could waste his or her time or cause him or her to lose valuable data.
5. If all else fails, find someone who works at company HQ and call or email them directly. Web search LinkedIn™ or company websites for corporate offices to find someone easily.

As a help desk manager, motivate your staff to help customers, not just close calls. Databases must have call exception tracking. There are always ways to improve both as a help desk professional and a caller.

FLIPPING THE SCRIPT

What happens when you're on the other side of the line? If you're a caller, sometimes you feel out of your depth. You're not a pro at computers, and if the person on the other end of the line can't understand your problem, it's frustrating.

I'll attempt to explain how help desk professionals can become more efficient at giving callers insight into how help desks work so that they will be more prepared to have a successful call completion.

Wait! You say you've heard that before? I agree, there are hundreds of companies out there that claim to provide more efficient help desk products. If so, why aren't help desks always helpful?

In one of my experiences, I found a software bug in an employee stock option trading program for a major US brokerage firm that was stealing funds from me. I found the problem by performing a reconciliation on my transaction history between my employee stock option (ESO) account and my brokerage account. Any first-year accounting student could easily follow the transactions. The error was obvious. It had been sixteen years since I took college accounting classes. I wasn't out to prove I was better than anyone else; I just wanted my money. Thousands of other people who have used this same type of ESO transaction have experienced the same problem—but was it possible *I* was the only one who noticed an incorrect transaction? Or did customer service constantly filter the complaints from the customers who called in?

The table below illustrates the transaction problem. Assume the per share market price was $10 higher than the cost. The unused money was never returned to me. Non-qualified ESOs must pay taxes on the difference between the market value and the exercise price taxed as ordinary income. Social Security tax in the US at the time was limited to the first $90,000 or so dollars. That limit has been raised several times. When the limit is reached, no more social security tax, which is 6.2% for individuals, and 12.4% for self-employed.

Illustrated Transaction Problem

Description	Costs used to "fund" the transaction including SS tax	Costs to fund the transaction without SS tax.
Exercise Cost	100 x $10 = $1000	100 x $10 = $1000
Taxes (Fed, Med, SS) on $1000	$357.50	$295.50
Over-estimated SS tax, unused money	$62	-$62

I reported the bug to the broker help desk, and each time the explanation was the same: "The adjustment credits should equal the debit funds," as if they were reading it from a script. But I kept telling them that my account transactions clearly showed that the two didn't add to the same total. They continued to reply that it "should" total the same. I like what Sammy Allred of

Austin's KVET 98.1 radio says, "Don't argue with an idiot because people watching can't tell the difference." There was no point in getting angry. After years of dealing with the help desk, I understood exactly what was happening.

Help desk professionals are not paid to think anymore, just paid to get the job done.

What is the job? Make the caller go away and close the call.

I finally realized how to prove it to them by placing myself in their shoes and thinking about how their customer service operation worked.

After two years of unproductive calls to the help desk and complaining to my employer's corporate treasury department (who also attempted to explain away the discrepancy and dismiss my complaint), I called on the afternoon of Friday, November 4, 2005, and told the help desk that I wasn't going away until I could speak to the right person and that I had proof there was a software bug.

You know how it is when you call the help desk: They need to verify your account before they listen to anything else. Yes, they do realize how intimidating that can be. But I refused to play fair. I refused to help them verify me until they promised to expedite my call to the highest level possible.

This time they put me in touch, right away, with a very experienced broker named Eric P. who also tried to tell me there was no problem. Again, I said, "I have heard that before, and with all due respect, the information he has is not accurate. I have proof, and I am not going away until he sees the evidence."

So, he allowed me to describe my proof. This time he actually listened and followed along in my account records. He asked if he could put me on hold. He was checking something. Fifteen minutes later he came back and said I was right. There indeed was a problem with the calculation software, and they had stolen approximately $2,900 from me since I began exercising my ESOs. He credited the amount to my account, and I asked him to also give me interest for the amount they withheld from me because I had no chance to invest that money. I was credited only $20 interest for the money they stole from me. I asked him if this was the first time the problem had been discovered, and he said yes. I could tell he was phrasing his answers very carefully; this type of problem could cause lots of bad publicity.

For the next several months, every time I exercised ESOs, I called the help desk and had them reverse the error and credit my account for the stolen money. Up to that point, I had nothing in writing, so the last time I called, I asked for it. I got them to send me a letter describing that they would fix their problem. I received the following letter by email from what appears to be a team leader (his name is different from the broker who helped me on the phone). Only the name of the financial institution, individual names, and phone numbers have been crossed out. All other text is original.

> *Dear Mr. Choate,*
>
> *Thank you for choosing XXXXXX Financial.*
> *Since receiving your inquiry through your company as to what is happening with funds being committed for stock option exercises, we have found the problem and have had it fixed.*
> *During your trades in the latter part of last year, funds would be journaled from the brokerage side of your account to the Stock Plan side, in anticipation of paying for both the option cost and the tax withholdings. The amount was dependent on the estimate of tax withholdings that we had on file from your company, so if your company ended up not withholding that amount, there should have been some leftover cash to be sent back to the brokerage account. Due to an operations issue, this did not always happen, leaving the funds in the Stock Plan portion of the account, viewable on your monthly statements, but not accessible online.*

I have received word from our operations department that the issue was found and fixed, and all funds journalled over to the Stock Plan portion of the account should journal back to the brokerage side to pay the company and to return the leftover amount if applicable.

I apologize for the inconvenience or confusion this may have caused. Please let me know if I can further assist you. My extension is listed below.

Sincerely,

Timothy MXXXXXXX
(xxx)8X8-5090 x123X
Mon-Fri 6:00AM-2:30PM PST
Financial Services Representative
XXXXXX Securities LLC

Excitedly, in April 2006, I performed a test option exercise and confirmed that the problem was indeed fixed.

Magic words: "Escalate my call to Level 3 support."

TAKING THESE CONCEPTS WITH YOU

I recently (2024) wanted to cancel a web subscription I no longer use because, as a retiree, I am on a fixed income. Unfortunately, the subscription auto-renewed before I could cancel, and the $169 six-month subscription fee was charged by credit card. I called the help desk and spoke to a nice customer service agent. I requested a refund because I no longer used the web service, and I was on a retirement fixed income. He explained that their policy didn't allow for a refund and there were no exceptions. I argued that their policy wasn't fair and promised I would do everything in my power to get a refund. I calmly spoke the magic words and asked to speak to a manager. He asked, "Am I to understand you are requesting to speak to a manager?" (It was a recorded line.) He was obviously well-trained to handle these types of calls, and since I was calm and didn't curse, he put me on hold, and in a few short minutes, he came back and said, "We have issued you a refund."

As a caller, if the answer doesn't make sense, ask to escalate to a senior representative, a team leader, supervisor, or manager, or use the magic words "escalate to level 3 tech support." If they refuse or stall, ask for a name or employee number and indicate that you will complete feedback surveys on this call. Also, if you have a good experience, I highly recommend that you provide positive feedback on the help desk survey. Good help desk talent is hard to find, and we have a duty to give feedback for good service, even if it only "meets expectations." Management at the help desk may have no other valid way to measure help-desk worker performance.

CHAPTER TWO
KEEP AN OPEN MIND

ONE DAY, I TRAVELED TO A CUSTOMER INSTALLATION IN Orlando which had one of our biggest system installations. The owner of the company was an outspoken industry leader. He had a lot of political clout and wasn't afraid to use it. He had already forced my company management to replace the entire system hardware once. He insisted on sending an army of experts from the factory to "fix" it after replacing the system did not resolve the problem. My company sent me.

The VAR system engineer had been onsite and incorrectly analyzed the problem, ultimately convincing the customer that the issue was a computer hardware problem. Since the hardware was provided by my company, we were the enemy. There were hundreds of other similar installations, and "none" were known to have reported to have the same problem. This was the largest type of single system installation my company had installed as the owner always insisted on having the biggest and the best of everything. Since it was different from similar installations, they concluded incorrectly that it had to be a hardware problem.

I sat down to analyze crash dump data on a huge green/white alternating stripe "zebra" paper printout looking for patterns that would explain the failure. There was an error message that indicated the central processing unit (CPU) had executed an illegal instruction[1]. So, in a way, it was a hardware problem: The software told the hardware to do something it wasn't designed to do[2]. It was an example of an explanation that wasn't logical.

But I wouldn't give up until I found the logical explanation.

I tried explaining this to the owner, but before I could finish explaining, I could see lightning bolts of anger flaring from his bloodshot eyes as he screamed, "Do you have any idea how much money this problem is costing me?" Because he thought the failure was in the hardware, he couldn't understand the analysis process to find the root cause. He wouldn't accept any additional delays and insisted on another system replacement and that I supervise the new installation.

I had no chance to defend my position. He called upper management and got what he wanted again. It took about three days to get the new system built, shipped, and installed. That was a record to my knowledge.

But replacing all the hardware for the second time still didn't resolve the failures, as I had predicted. It was after this that I had the most unpleasant tongue-lashing of my life by a representative of the owner. I was threatened that, if I didn't fix the problem immediately, not only would I no longer have a job at my company, but I couldn't set foot on any of his associations' properties worldwide for the rest of my life. *At least I would still have*

---

1. Many people misinterpret this error message. The error does not mean the CPU illegally executed an instruction as commonly thought, it means that the CPU was executing valid instructions until it got one that it could not execute because the instruction to the CPU was not in the library of legal instructions.
2. While this was a serious problem at the time, it's not something that would happen in modern computers today. Early computer development didn't have the tools or the benefit of foresight to provide protected memory segments. They didn't have privilege mechanisms for each memory segment. Modern computers have security functions that prevent tasks from accessing the memory assigned to another task.

my horse, I thought. It occurred to me I might also have to defend myself from physical attack. I walked outside and came up with a plan. I had to have the customer on my side to get my work done. I called upon my training in Interpersonal Communications and Situational Leadership.

A LOGICAL STEP FORWARD

Though this story illustrates a worst-case scenario, most help desk professionals are expected to know the answers to difficult problems daily. As mentioned in the last chapter, many people who call the help desk are already angry. It's your job to find a solution.

You can never fully anticipate the unexpected, but you can develop a process for solving problems that no one else has ever faced. You can apply thinking, listening, and logical rules to almost any problem, both technical and interpersonal.

Learn to recognize a pattern where no pattern has existed before.

Conversely, insisting that missing data fit a pre-established standard closes the rational mind to other possibilities. If you make a list of *all* known causes and systematically rule out each item on the list and it still remains a mystery, then the true answer must either not be on the list or one of the methods you previously used was faulty.

It's a system that people have used for thousands of years, and it works.

When you deal with customers, however, not everyone uses the same method for solving problems. It's common for customers to skip steps when they're frustrated. One of the most infuriating problems is when you're right but the customer insists that you're wrong. Sometimes they even go over your head to force management to do the wrong thing to solve the problem at the great expense of time and money.

WRESTLING WITH CUSTOMERS

I approached the owner's rep and said I needed twenty-four hours. I outlined my logical plan to investigate the problem and steps to define corrective action. I explained that getting angry didn't help and that I had the resources of the company at my disposal to help me as needed. I told them I needed their help also and asked for permission to talk to the staff using the computer.

The most experienced user was a know-it-all type. He barked orders, telling everyone how to use computers and why they're unreliable pieces of junk. I sure didn't have any problems getting him to talk. He kept saying he knew the problem, but no one would listen to him. He said it was a software problem. He hadn't heard the theory regarding the illegal instruction, and I tried to explain it to him, but I soon realized he had the attention span of a five-year-old.

As he loudly explained how the problem occurred—kind of like a gorilla pounding on his chest to impress other jungle animals—he parked his finger on the keyboard. He said there was a bad connection in the printer because, just before the system usually crashed, the printer wouldn't work when he pressed the print invoice key. He actually believed that the keyboard print key had a switch that connected a wire inside the keyboard to the printer that initiated printing. The VAR had a custom keyboard that reprogrammed the F10 key to the print function for the invoice application. But the F10 was covered up with a label that said "Print."

Most folks don't know how computers work. When a key is pressed, the keyboard logic scans which key is pressed, decodes it, and sends an interrupt to the CPU, sort of like when a child pulls on his mother's skirt when her attention is on something else. Just like how the mom reads the child's needs, the CPU reads the users' needs by reading the keyboard status port. It then captures the key codes, decoding their meaning to execute pre-programmed responses.

The print key functioned as a two-character keyboard command. For the print function, the CPU queued a file read command operation and then transferred the file to the printer device port, one character at a time. Interruptions at the CPU are prioritized, similar to how a parent may prioritize which child gets undivided attention when more than one child demands attention. Basically, lower-priority tasks must wait. Some impatient users interpret this waiting period as disdain from the computer. But the computer can only do what it is told to do. It has limitations.

In this case, the user parked his finger on the print key, which made handling higher-priority tasks harder for the other users because the keyboard was programmed to sense when a key was held down and automatically send the same interrupt to the CPU repeatedly. The CPU was so busy that it only had time to save the keyboard key in a temporary buffer while it waited for time to read the buffered keyboard command and process it.

It just so happens that the buffer organization was defined by the software program, a.k.a. the code. Still, the program didn't anticipate the large number of keystrokes sent automatically, especially since the print key was a two-character key. In contrast, most other keys were only one character, so the buffer never overflowed. When the buffer overflowed without notice, the print key codes corrupted the first few bytes of the main program called the common business-oriented language (COBOL) Run-time program. The two-character F10 key hexadecimal code was executed instead of the expected instruction. The print key was interpreted as a branch and load workspace pointer (BLWP) instruction[3].

---

3. This response was more common in older models of computers. It's an instruction used in assembly language programming for some microprocessors.

The designer of the 990 computer instruction set, a computer pioneer by the name of Moise Adney, named this instruction "Branch and Load Workspace Pointer," but everyone except me called it the "blowup" instruction. Since I was a cowboy, I called it the "bullwhip" instruction.

My friend, Stu, used to say, "You can always tell the pioneers by the arrows in their back." The BLWP instruction wasn't supposed to be there and had altered the CPU instruction pointer randomly, sometimes executing wrong instructions that would cause the "illegal instruction" error or cause the CPU to just freeze or hang, a.k.a. "crash."

The COBOL Run-time program is like the mother to all the child programs in the system. When the mother crashed, all the child programs stopped working.

As a temporary workaround, I reconfigured the system to launch new mother programs automatically for each child program, so when the buffer overflowed, it only crashed one mother and one child while all the others kept running. This bought us more time, and shortly after, other users within the VAR network association had the same problem. The focus of the analysis turned to the software, and the buffer overflow programming bug was found.

Since the problem was not a hardware problem, and since the customer interference partly caused an additional delay, my company sent an invoice to the customer for the onsite service I provided, but it was never paid. We didn't think it would be.

MEMORY PROBLEMS

The BLWP instruction calls subroutines to a new workspace, so it not only jumps to a new subroutine but also sets up a set of new registers for that subroutine to use. In essence, the subroutine has its own local environment without interfering with the registers of the calling program.

When was the last time you had trouble with your computer's inability to multi-task? If you worked with computers after the early 1980s, you probably don't remember the days when computer processes had more quirks than they do now. But it's because of major problems like the one I just mentioned that there is protective memory today.

Memory protection ensures that the operating system isolates one process from another. It prevents processes from overlapping each other and overwriting other processes. Too many processes working at once could corrupt data or code belonging to another process and ultimately lead the system to crash. If a malicious program enters a system without memory protection, the overwriting could potentially corrupt files and even lead to security breaches.

Today, protective memory is on every computer. Most systems are required to multi-task for basic operations, and without protective memory, computers would crash frequently. It took the creativity of engineers in the early days of computers to find a solution to the problem, and it's why you won't see that same issue today.

SEEKING THE CUSTOMER SOLUTION

Computers have become more sophisticated, but there are always new problems and new people who don't understand how computers work. Finding the right balance between knowledgeable communication and empathy for customers is a tough line to walk. Just because you may know much more than the caller doesn't mean you can easily explain the solutions to problems over the phone.

Dealing with difficult customers is equal parts logical and emotional. You need to find solutions to problems without letting bias cloud your judgment while simultaneously giving customers the space to air out their grievances. Below are some methods to help you find a balance.

Cultivating a Critical Thinking Mentality

As a help desk professional, caller, engineer, or student, refining your creativity and critical thinking skills is essential to finding solutions to problems. Here are some suggestions to increase those skills.

See a Pattern

Pattern recognition is vitally important in determining intelligence. Patterns are in language, culture, and especially science and math. What we see as critical thinking is the application of pattern recognition. The faster we learn from experience and adapt to new situations, the faster we can understand complex ideas and formulate reason.

Intelligence is the ability to adapt those problem-solving skills into replicable methods. It's what many in the science community have dubbed "the scientific method," and it's something you've probably seen before on your own. You form a theory, test that theory, gather evidence and data, and adjust your theory based on the results. Once you see the pattern enough times, you commit it to memory and base new theories on what you've learned.

It's easy to believe that, once you've mastered several patterns, you can find solutions to nearly all problems by applying those patterns. But patterns change. The tricky part is being adaptable and having an open mind.

New developments in technology and daily life require new problem-solving solutions.

Look at Information Critically

As you've seen in this chapter, a lot of people get caught up in thinking they know all the answers. If something stops working, most people go to their most recent experience to find a solution. The problem is that different situations have new challenges. Not every solution to an old issue will fit a new problem.

Think more critically by breaking down problems into premises and conclusions. Is there a logical connection between the evidence and your conclusion? Do you know when your theory is guaranteed a solution, or are you assuming that one step leads to the next? And, if you are making an assumption, are you eliminating any biases you might have from previous experiences? Using your experience to come to a logical conclusion is how we learn to think critically, but not all our experience is relevant. You might need to make changes based on new information.

Rule Out Methods that Aren't Helpful

Once you have a list of every solution you can think of, take a knife to it. What conclusions just don't make sense? Any solutions that don't apply to your situation or simply don't involve all the same moving parts should be eliminated.

Next, narrow down your assumptions to isolate which solution *does* make sense. As Sherlock Holmes put it, "When you have eliminated the impossible, whatever remains, however improbable, must be the truth[4]." Sometimes the solution you find isn't one that you'd expected. In my experience working with computers (and especially in daily life), I find that unusual solu-

---

4. Arthur Conan Doyle, *The Sign of Four* (London: Spencer Blackett, 1890), Chap. 6.

are often the answers that stick. Complex problems require complex problem-solving, even if the solution is simple.

Hostile Negotiation

The second piece to the customer problem-solving puzzle is communicating effectively. Working with customers isn't easy. A hostile situation can make or break you, and for some people, it feels like you'll never get the hang of keeping a strong stance when talking to hostile people. But, as a help desk professional, student, or engineer, you'll eventually need to learn how to adapt, if you're not already using those skills.

The good news is that anyone can learn how to talk with people. Here are some methods to improve how you deal with hostile people.

Develop Situational Relationship Awareness

THE BROADER RELATIONSHIPS CUSTOMERS HAVE WITH their employees and peers say a lot about them, and it's the first indicator for establishing situational relationship awareness. Small signs, like how callers leverage their intelligence, how they approach problems strategically, and how they develop social relationships tell you how to transform opportunities to suit your advantage.

First, identify the context of the situation and the relationship dynamics of the team. Power imbalances in employer-employee relationships can give you a clue about how they will talk to you. Some people, regardless of their position in a company, will feel a loss of power when they need to call someone to help them, which can make people angry. As a customer service expert, you'll probably see the problems people have with communicating when they're frustrated. Recognizing their triggers early by seeing how they react to you and the people around them can help you discover a better strategy for handling tough customers.

Learn Personality Models

DEALING WITH DIFFICULT CUSTOMERS INVOLVES understanding how people operate. If you struggle to deal with hostile people, knowing the basic personality types can give you a better idea of how you can change your approach. Here are some of the most common personality models and how you can apply them.

- The Myers-Briggs Type Indicator (MBTI)[5]

The (MBTI) personality model breaks personalities down into sixteen personality types based on introverts vs. extroverts, sensing vs. intuition, thinking vs. feeling, and judging vs. perceiving. Based on the results, you can break people into analysts, diplomats, sentinels, and explorers. Knowing whether a customer is more drawn to logical or emotional approaches can help you present information in a way that will appeal to them better. You can also find better methods of teaching people based on their personality types.

- DISC Assessment[6]

This assessment breaks down behaviors into four personality traits: dominance (D), influence (I), steadiness (S), and conscien-

---

5. You can find more information on the Myers-Briggs Type Indicator at https://www.16personalities.com/
6. You can find more information on DISC assessments here: https://www.discprofile.com/

(C). More dominant personalities can better relate to direct and honest communication. On the other hand, steady customers may prefer a calmer and more patient approach that focuses on a lasting relationship with you.

- The Big Five Personality Traits[7]

The Big Five personality traits are based on openness, conscientiousness, extraversion, agreeableness, and neuroticism. They are similar to the DISC assessment personalities but focus on a more emotional approach. Customers with high agreeableness are more likely to value harmony and will be more receptive to polite and friendly interactions. On the other hand, those with a neurotic personality are more likely to perceive threats and may need an approach that focuses more on reducing anxiety and finding long-term solutions.

Develop Negotiation Skills

NEGOTIATION IS A GAME OF STRATEGY. IT'S CHESS played out in real time. But negotiation is easy when you learn about with whom you're dealing Validate the power you have and what power the other party has to facilitate changes.

Gain as much information as possible before you speak. Analyze the intonation of the speaker. Are they angry, frustrated, or easy to talk to? If they talk with you in a commanding voice, change your response to make communication as effective as possible. If you can see the caller during your conversation, pick up on nonverbal cues, such as arm crossing or eye contact, to see

---

7. You can find more information on the Big Five personality traits here: Gerald Matthews, Ian J. Deary, and Martha C. Whiteman, *Personality Traits*, 3rd ed. (Cambridge: Cambridge University Press, 2009).

how the other person engages. Sometimes you can hear nonverbal cues through the phone[8]. Mimic both their intonation and their nonverbal cues. Mimicking people lets them know that you're listening and engaged.

You can also ease the tension by using "we" language. Remember, you're both finding a solution to a problem and if you frame your responses in a "we are in this together" tone of voice, the person you're talking to will be more likely to listen. You're also much more likely to remain calm if you feel like you're working *with* the caller instead of *against* them.

Finally, look for a win-win solution by satisfying both your caller's and your needs. One of the best wins you can give your caller is trust; if they can trust you, they can communicate openly. In some cases, callers are more likely to give you and your company their business simply because they feel they can trust the staff. You're ultimately finding a solution that focuses on their interests, not just on positions you can take to make a sale. It may take creative problem-solving, but there's always a solution when negotiating correctly.

---

8. For example, you can often tell if someone is smiling by how they talk. You can also tell if someone is standing or sitting based on the speed of their voice; people who pace tend to speak faster than those who are sitting.

CHAPTER THREE
CHANGE ON THE HORIZON

EVENTUALLY, IT BECAME VERY DIFFICULT TO KEEP trained people with the right personalities on the same help desk for many years. One of the reasons for turnover in skilled workers was the increasing number of verbally abusive customers. To be clear, I believe people aren't naturally abusive, but many think it's necessary to behave that way to get the help desk's attention when technical support can't satisfy the user's complaint. The individual complaining may have experienced other help desk employees at other firms who wouldn't know a shorted fuse from a burned-out light bulb[1].

There weren't always enough help desk agents to answer calls during busy days. When the help desk was busy with other customers and the buzzer on the wall indicated a customer phone call hadn't been answered within five rings, the administrative

---

1. Usually, if something is "shorted," it is defective, but fuses become "open" when the fuse rating is exceeded or damaged. If you want to confuse a rookie engineer with little practical hands-on experience, ask them to check if their fuse is shorted.

assistant would answer the phone. Within ten rings, it was automatically transferred to the manager on duty.

One Christmas Eve afternoon, the few of us managing the phones were all very busy and the administrative assistant answered the phone on about the tenth ring. The customer spoke to her using very abusive language for taking so long to answer the phone. The verbal abuse was so bad that, in a short time, she started crying and hung up on the jerk. I called the customer back to tell him that he didn't have a right to be abusive on the phone and that unless he apologized, he wouldn't get any help. I'm not sure if he was on drugs, drinking, or just having a bad day, but he had no right to abuse her that way. And by golly, I did not care how much money the customer had spent with my company or about the "customer is always right" policy, he couldn't get away with being verbally abusive. I told him to call back when he could behave himself and we would help him. It turned out he had a very simple question, and we were easily able to help him once he called back. He wasn't used to anyone standing up to challenge him. I took a risk speaking to him the way I did. I never got into any trouble for it, and I earned the respect of many co-workers that day.

THE PERSONALITY THAT STICKS

Dealing with difficult customers is one of the most taxing parts of working at the help desk. It takes a specific type of personality to handle some of the more difficult calls. Anyone can learn how to work at the help desk, but it takes time and practice. I had to learn how to survive at a help desk the hard way.

Our work areas were arranged in one large shared square pit built using Herman-Miller™ modular furniture. The administrative assistants were in the middle with half-height walls and modular furniture. They could answer the phone and see which tech support agent wasn't on the phone. They'd then transfer the call to the first person available who could handle the call. From where we sat, we could easily see everyone in the pit from our work areas at the perimeter of the pit.

There was no delay for a computer to retrieve data from a database to see who was available. The data was right in front of our eyes in hardcopy and at our fingertips. Sometimes we got so busy as soon as we hung up the phone that it would ring again. I couldn't bear to use the phone without those fancy hands-free headsets. My fear of my inability to solve a problem quickly faded; I had no time to consider what I might not know!

This lack of fear was to become one of my greatest strengths as a help desk expert. My confidence soon grew when I realized that, if I didn't know the answer, I knew how to either find the answer or find someone else who did[2].

Sometimes, the fear of making a mistake immobilizes productive thoughts and/or actions, especially if you are likely to be caught, humiliated, and/or punished for the mistake. Whenever you aren't sure what to do first, make a list of possible options. Even if you choose the wrong one first, you'll soon get a clue about possible correct options. Doing something, even if it's wrong, is better than doing nothing. When learning a process, write everything down, document every step, and review the steps after you have completed the call. Imagine different situations and different optional steps so you will be prepared for the next time. This is also referred to in the industry of systems engineering as the Design of Experiments (D.O.E.) process.

The key is always wanting to improve yourself and the experience of your customers. If you recognize something in yourself that needs improvement, take the time to adapt.

---

2. Later, I learned that human behavioral models called this level of realization *self-efficacy* or *self-actualization*.

THE SEARCH FOR SUCCESS

We had a printed list of help desk representative names, their desk phone numbers, and sometimes their pager IDs at each of our workstations. All books were hard copies; we had no electronic books or manuals at the time, and we had many stacks of computer printouts on our shelves. It was a well-documented process that took time but was ultimately worth the time it took to put everything on paper.

As the help desk evolved and expanded, we had fewer highly skilled people willing to transfer to the help desk team, even temporarily. So, we had no choice but to accept underqualified people to answer the telephone, take call notes, and escalate the call to a specialist.

There were many pressures by management to improve the effectiveness of the help desk. Some of the metrics included the following: the number of calls, the number of calls per person, the number of calls per customer, and the type of calls received—such as hardware calls, software calls, or simply a documentation question call. Call exceptions occurred often: Was the call for a new problem that needed engineering action, or was it a user problem that indicated that the training or documentation provided needed improvement? In the help desk's early days, we didn't even take written records of the type of call and type of problem. But, to justify increasing the staff budget for the helpdesk, we needed to document this data.

As more data came in, it became apparent that we could use this data to predict what type of calls we may have on new products. We could also train underqualified people to handle those types of calls using a checklist or flowchart that eventually turned into a script. Perhaps 75% of the calls could be handled this way, and we could significantly reduce our labor budget.

Documenting *every* call manually on a paper form with details of the problem and the solution became a nuisance for help desk professionals. Eventually, we hired administrative assistants to tally the data from our paper forms into a master sheet. Each team member provided feedback on additional fields to print on the form to reduce time when filling out the forms. We made the call forms in triplicate for ourselves, the physical file, and the database entry. There were many errors in the database records. The errors had to be found and corrected manually but no one realized the need for this, so the dirty work fell onto the manager, who delegated it to the help desk.

What a waste of time, sitting there going over records that were typed incorrectly.

Finding a hidden pattern was useful because it could lead to a change for the better. But, at that time, there were no other options for accurate data collection. For the help desk to succeed as an organization, it had to collect data about what it did, organize it, and present it to management to justify its own existence.

It makes you wonder; how much time was wasted on doing work when work was needed elsewhere.

THE CO-WORKER HACK

My weakest ability was my tact (or lack thereof) in asking for urgent help from co-workers, and I was reminded of this every performance review. I, however, the highest of highest achievers, was so valuable to the company that there were never any punishments or threats of punishment if I didn't correct my tactless nature toward co-workers.

I *did*, however, fix my tact problem, and the skill became very useful in my later career. My favorite way of tactfully asking for help was to first use flattery to butter them up, and then ask, "If it's not too much trouble," could they drop everything they are doing to help me solve a customer's problem?

. . .

Follow-Up, Follow-Through, And Do It Right the First Time!

I developed a very successful general rule of engagement with co-workers that I have used in many different companies and positions.

Follow Up:

Follow-up means politely reminding a co-worker of a promised delivery when they haven't yet delivered what they promised. You can disguise the follow-up phone call as a friendly check on the status to see if they need anything else from you and remind them you still need their help. Include a reference to what importance or urgency level remains.

Follow-Through:

Follow-through means honoring your promised commitments and delivering on time. If you can't deliver what or when you promised, let the person know as soon as possible. Don't wait until the last minute. People depend on answers, and they may need to use alternative plans to get answers if you can't provide them.

Sometimes, the right answer comes from someone else, or you can discover it on your own. In these cases, you have a duty to inform the person you are waiting on that you no longer need their help; don't waste any more of his or her valuable time. Show concern for their time and prior commitments. You can easily destroy a trusting working relationship by getting the reputation of asking for urgent assistance from many people at the same time and wasting their valuable time. Not showing any appreciation for their efforts because you got the answer, or you no longer needed it and neglected to tell them is a great way to get on someone's bad side.

Likewise, be helpful to others when they ask, but don't do their work for them. I prefer showing people how to research the answer if they have the time and patience. Help them understand that you have important work to do. Helping them can have a positive impact on your delivery schedule, if applicable. Sometimes, they will realize they could find the answer themselves without bothering you. Or they may realize they didn't really need the information that badly.

In many cases, the urgency of the situation justifies the work interruption, and being the best person to help is part of your job description.

Do It Right the First Time

"Do it right the first time" has become an overused cliché in the last twenty-five years. My position is that it always costs more to re-do it than to do it right the first time. The costs are tallied in product delays, labor costs, and human resource costs.

Product developers should also take responsibility for the quality of their work. Product developers should help their downstream consumers understand what the problem is, how a product works, and how to troubleshoot the product if something doesn't seem right. Developers should also have design reviews during development at several stages to ensure all the stakeholders understand what is expected, which gives them the opportunity for constructive feedback. Everything should be documented, including how sub-components interact with main components. Each component should have a support owner to field questions from stakeholders and downstream consumers, even internal ones.

By troubleshooting the product development early and using all the resources necessary to make your product more effective, you can avoid changing the product all over again.

CHAPTER FOUR
FORM, FIT, AND FUNCTION

My first assignment on the hotline was as a product support specialist for a high-speed printer from a supplier named Printronix. They replaced the OEM skins with skins that used our company branding. This allowed us to compete with other computer systems offering high-speed printers. Our firm manufactured dot matrix printers[1], but some customers needed a high-volume high-speed printer. I went to a one-week factory training school in Los Angeles, CA to learn more about their processes.

The Printronix printers were drum printers that printed one line at a time. They had a rapidly spinning metal drum with raised characters on hammers; an electronic hammer relay timed to fire when the desired letter was at the right position, and a carbon ribbon left an impression on a multi-part continuous feed paper. Heavy electrical motors advanced the paper as each line of characters printed. The printer included an adjustable machined metal platen bar behind the continuously fed paper to maintain tension.

---

1. They were character-based dot-matrix printers that printed only one character at a time.

Since Printronix was an industrial-scale company, hardcopy memorandums of change notices were created to notify the OEMs of any changes to the product. There was a classification of changes that were contractually reviewed and accepted conditionally after testing to ensure the change met the requirements of the intended purpose. Any change that affected form, fit, or function required review and conditional approval for acceptance.

Since I was the designated support specialist, I received and reviewed all the product change notices from the manufacturer of the printers. One day, I saw there was a notice for a change in the supplier of the platen. It was tagged as a change that did not affect form, fit, or function and was only modified to reduce cost.

After the printer with the new cost-reduced platen went into production and shipped to our customers, I noticed that we received more complaints than normal for printouts that had linespacing abnormalities. Normally, customers expected consistent spacing between each printed line. Abnormally, the customer complained that some lines missed the space between separate lines.

By tracing the serial number history, I determined the printer serial numbers experiencing the spacing issues included the cost-reduced platen. I retrieved the change notice document which included the phone number to call for additional information. I called HQ for the printer help desk and told them about the customer complaints. They explained the original platen was manufactured in-house, but a new local supplier was found in Los Angeles to reduce cost. I asked for and received the phone number of the supplier for the cost-reduced platen. I called the company and spoke with their engineering manager who was also the owner since it was a small company. He gave me a history of the platen change.

They had started a small machine shop in the garage of the owner's home and had aggressively sought new jobs. The owner approached local businesses in LA asking for opportunities to become suppliers of machined components to help them reduce production costs. When they approached Printronix down the street from them, the specifications for the platen were shared by the purchasing department. The startup machinist company manufactured some samples and gave them to the company for testing.

The internal testing compared the sample platens to the legacy platens and found that they met the requirements, so they approved switching to the local third-party supplier. Purchasing placed, the order and the new platens went into production. What they didn't know was that the test procedure used to qualify the new platens didn't include testing for line-spacing anomalies[2].

FIND THE CONNECTION

What's the moral of the story? The notifications you get from suppliers may not be entirely accurate. They don't always make a positive change for your production. It takes a problem solver to find solutions to problems.

The problem is that many companies don't look deeply into who can find the right solutions to problems or they don't follow the rules to increase the value of their products. It's important to consistently test products before releasing them to the public. Companies have a responsibility to make sure their customers get the best products possible. That's only possible with constant checking.

When implementing your own systems, consider the following to maintain proper form, fit, and function.

- When sourcing components or systems from third

---

2. See Chapter 8, Being Tense is Better! for more information about troubleshooting on this problem type.

parties, receive written notice of any and all changes to the manufacture of those products from the third party.
- Purchasing contracts should require timely written notice of all changes.
- Changes to form, fit, or function should be highlighted.
- Samples of the products containing changes should be tested under extreme test conditions representing real-life operating conditions.
- Acceptance of changes should be conditional upon successful testing of samples.
- Product support personnel should review all written change notices.
- Purchasing departments should document all requirements when requesting samples from alternate sources.
- Once solutions are found, update the form, fit, or function definitions that need improvement.

WEAKEST LINK

Unfortunately, it's the small things that go unnoticed most often. Poor quality in the most basic procedures has ground entire systems to a stop. Sometimes the biggest problems are the easiest to solve if you take your problem-solving seriously.

The following is a true story that illustrates how following poor-quality procedures can cause serious problems.

Monday, April 30, 1979, the day after Daylight Savings Time began, and an hour of my morning daylight was lost. I was in the process of moving from one apartment complex to another, and my phone rang; the only thing left in my old apartment was the phone (a push-button landline), broom, dustpan, cleaning rags, and liquid cleaner. I worked alone, and I just finished cleaning up.

FORM, FIT, AND FUNCTION   51

By noon, I still hadn't had lunch. I almost didn't answer it. I don't even know why I decided to leave the phone in the old apartment or why I plugged it in.

Wireless phones hadn't been invented. I grew up in the age of rotary dial phones. It used pulse dialing. There were two conductors called TIP and RING connecting the phone company network to a personal landline phone. A switch in the handset controlled the phone status of on-hook and off-hook, which was managed by the phone handset's microphone and earpiece on opposite ends of the handset. When the on-hook mode was valid, the phone could ring for incoming calls. When the off-hook status was valid, the rotary dialer pulsed the wire to indicate the number sequence was connected to another personal code. For push-button phone service (a.k.a. Direct Distance Dialing or DDD), when pressing the number keys 0 through 9, #, or *, the phone generated dual frequencies on the copper wire connecting the phone handset to the phone company substation. Central phone control circuits then decoded the frequencies and routed calls by decoding the ten-digit phone number into a three-digit area code starting with a number greater than 1, a local two-digit service provider or local exchange network, and a five-digit personal calling code. This replaced the old seven-digit phone number system where the first two characters specified the local network followed by five numeric digits, which identified the exchange and personal code. International calls required a first digit of 0, and long-distance calls required a first digit of 1 in those days.

Since this was the first day I'd had off since joining the help desk and knowing how much the help desk depended on me, I suppose a sense of pride caused me to plug in the phone. I'd expected someone would need me to come to the rescue and answer a quick question. I had no idea I would soon go on the longest trouble call of my life up to that point, nor that this trip would have a profound impact on the help desk industry (at least profound in *my* little part of the world).

· · ·

CROSSING LEAGUES

My boss's boss, Bob Ledbetter, was on the phone. Bob had a very calm inflection in his voice, as he usually did—he could easily be a church pastor. He said, "Mike, this is Bob. How are you doing?" I told him I had the day off to move between apartments. He asked if I was finished moving. I told the truth: I mentioned I was minutes from finishing at the old apartment and ready to turn in the key. He wasted no time, and asked, "Have you ever been to London?"

I was shocked; I certainly was not expecting that question. I said, "No."

In an encouraging tone of voice, he said, "You would like to go to London, wouldn't you?" Well, without knowing when this trip to England would happen, I eagerly told Bob someday I wished I would have the opportunity. He then asked in a more hurried voice "You do have a passport, don't you?" I barely had a chance to say yes when he interrupted and said, "Well, good news. Your wish has come true. Your plane leaves in four hours. We have a customer hardware problem over there and you are the best person available. Pack for one week, and you'll get the details after you arrive."

I objected, saying I could probably solve it over the phone if I knew what the symptoms were.

He said there was no time to explain. "Don't miss your plane."

Eighteen smoky-cabin hours later, I arrived at Gatwick Airport in London after flying first class on Braniff Airlines with a connection in D/FW. Cigarette, pipe, and cigar smoking were still allowed on international flights in those days. I was young and due to my martial arts training, was in excellent physical condition. I also had red hair, a full beard, a mustache, and blue eyes. Since only 0.17% of people have both red hair and blue eyes, I

FORM, FIT, AND FUNCTION 53

should be easy to spot in a crowd. My biological mother, my half-brother, my half-sister, and their kids had the same shade of red hair. Not my son, his hair color took after his mother. Smokey cabins didn't bother me because everyone in my family used tobacco, so I was used to it. I was too excited to sleep and hadn't slept for over twenty-four hours anyway. It was 6 am, Tuesday, local Austin time, and 1 pm, Tuesday, London time, on May 1.

When I landed, I saw a guy holding a sign with my name on it near baggage claim, and we sat down for tea. Tim was the local field service engineer, one of several people who worked on stabilizing the new computer installation for six months. There were many problems, one after another, and the software was finally ready for release[3]. It seemed they were successful in getting everything working, but, after anywhere from one to five days, the system stopped for an unknown reason. The frustrated customer didn't want to waste any more time. They were told that the best guy from Texas was coming to fix it[4].

As Tim described the problem, I began analyzing the cause. The failure was very intermittent. The customer had been very understanding and forgiving, but that was only because the delivery deadline hadn't yet been reached. But the deadline was fast approaching. We had to get it fixed within one week, or they would kick the system out on the street. I was still fired up about being in London. A few hours earlier, I was in a T-shirt, dirty and sweaty, and now I was in a famous international airport with the weight of my company on my shoulders. I didn't even know what

---

3. This was a pilot installation for potentially hundreds of system installations.
4. I can't tell you how many times I was asked if I rode a horse. One of my former help desk experts, Adolf R, and I laughed about going to a customer site, pulling out pocketknives, and scraping the horse manure from the bottom of our boots into his trash can as we listened to the initial reports about some problem we were asked to fix. It just so happened, that I had my boots on, and I had forgotten to clean them before I left, and I really did have some old horse manure on the heel of my right boot. I made a mental note to pick the right time to scrape my boots to make the biggest impression.

the system looked like. So, I suggested going to the customer site right away, and maybe I could get lucky.

We got my rental car, and I almost killed myself leaving the parking lot: I forgot they drove on the wrong side of the road. We got to a warehouse where the computer was installed, and I was introduced as the guy from Texas. "Do you ride a horse to work?" they asked with big smiles on their faces.

"Sure do," I said. "Where is your trash can? I need to clean my boots."

The Price of Imperfection

The system was in a new low-profile rack with a desktop surface. I had never seen one before. It had the rack-mounted foot-tall computer chassis installed which slid in and out for servicing in the lower bay. It also had a foot-tall disk drive with a single removable fourteen-inch platter, also on slide-mounts, in the upper bay on the right-hand side of the desk.

The first thing I noticed was that the CPU circuit boards appeared slightly loosened from their backplane connector, i.e., they weren't fully seated or inserted. I asked Tim for a large screwdriver. According to the operator, the system was running but was never stable for long. I tapped on the side of the CPU chassis with the handle of the screwdriver, and the system instantly crashed, becoming unresponsive (we call that condition "locked up"). These guys must have thought I was crazy. They probably thought, "This bloke walks in, and in a few seconds makes the system crash. Who does he think he is? He is supposed to be fixing the bloody thing!"

I asked if that was the same type of lock-up they had seen before. They said it was similar, but they weren't all alike. I pressed on the pull tabs that held the CPU boards in and heard the familiar *snap* to indicate that the board had settled into the fully seated or inserted position. By instinct, I pulled the boards out to give them a visual inspection and noticed that several socketed components appeared loose in their "DIP" (Dual-inline-pin) socket. So, I pushed them all the way in and found several components were loose and close to breaking a good connection.

When the factory does all the engineering and quality testing, there are metal shipping brackets that hold the boards in place so the boards can't loosen. It also dampens vibration. The new desk rack was the first one that had the disk drive and the CPU chassis in the same cabinet bay. The new software ran longer duration bursts, which caused much more disk activity than earlier versions. More disk activity meant more vibration. The vibration caused the boards and socket components to gradually wiggle their connections loose, causing intermittent electrical connection, which resulted in unpredictable system malfunctions. The failure type depends upon the type of computer operation in progress at the time of the broken connection and which connection or combination of connections of the many thousand possible combinations breaks first. A system is only as strong as its least reliable component or connection. Just like a chain is only as strong as its weakest link.

MAKING THE CONNECTION

I pointed to the shipping brackets lying beneath the chassis and said, "The brackets are not installed! That's causing the problem."

Tim protested: "These are called shipping brackets because they're only used during shipping. The installation manual says to remove them and leave them off. Every system we have installed always has those brackets removed, and they never had this problem."

I asked him to show me the installation manual. I didn't remember that process step. Lo and behold, he was right. I told Tim I would feel more confident if we could install the brackets.

That was the way I had always seen the systems tested in the factory, and if it failed, we could troubleshoot the failure the hard way. We could let the system run overnight, and if it still failed, at least we would have ruled the brackets out as a potential cause of failure. As he installed the brackets, I leaned against the wall next to the trash can and scraped that horse manure from my boots. He saw no harm in this proposed course of action. Fifteen minutes after I arrived on site, we left for the evening.

On Wednesday, when we arrived in the morning, we were greeted with the news that the system hadn't malfunctioned even once overnight. But this has happened before, so the customer was very skeptical. So, I said, "Let's do the screwdriver test[5]."

I got the screwdriver and tapped the system—hard—all over, and it never failed. Well, word about what I'd done got back to our headquarters in Dallas, and the response was disbelief. When I asked if I could come home, they told me not to return until the customer was convinced it was truly fixed. No one believed I could fix it in fifteen minutes with such a simple and obvious fix.

I called my expert co-workers, told them what I'd done, and asked if they were working on any other similar problems. When they said they were, I told them to install the shipping brackets to see if the problem went away. In a short time, failing systems showed up all over the world, and the shipping bracket fix seemed to fix them all. I recommended that we send a formal document

---

5. I worked part-time in a TV/radio repair shop during college and had an electronics class during high school. One of the most common repairs was to re-apply solder to broken joints. It was easy to find broken joints or poor electrical connections by tapping on the circuit board with a large screwdriver's plastic handle while observing the working or failing pattern. I would tap all over the board until I located the most sensitive place. Then I inspected all the connections until I found one that looked like the molten metal didn't flow around the component correctly. Lead was commonly used in solder because it was soft, a good electrical conductor, and melted easily, but contamination often caused corrosion. Sometimes a wire brush removed the corrosion before reapplying the solder. Lead solder is still used in modern electronics and has become more purified and less susceptible to failure.

to all our service offices which led to the immediate creation and release of "Field Bulletin FB-001." Because some installers threw away the brackets after reaching their destination, a kit part number was created that included the brackets and the fasteners. This led to the release of the revised FSB-001A.

Management began to ask a lot of questions: "Why did it take someone from Austin such a short time to find a fix to such an easy problem?" and "How can we prevent other problems in the future?" Soon, this FSB communication method became so valuable that a new group was created to compose and distribute these documents worldwide while maintaining the mailing lists and fax phone numbers. Depending on the urgency, some were faxed and others were put in snail mail.

A London Jaunt

Management made me extend my stay in London for a second week. I traveled around and visited museums, parks, and pubs, ultimately developing a powerful taste for fish and chips. There was something about it when they served it in a newspaper. I had a jolly good time.

During one of my frequent jaunts on Friday, May 4 at about 10 pm, I went down to SOHO, the red-light district, and found an underground pub. As I walked down the stairs with my cowboy boots and hat, a table of rugby players insisted that I join them for a few pints and lead them in singing "You Picked a Fine Time to Leave Me Lucille[6]" repeatedly. The song was made famous internationally by recording star Kenny Rogers in 1977. Obviously, my appearance shouted, "Texan—pick on me." All Texans ride horses and sit around all day singing Western songs, therefore, I must know the words to the song.

---

6. Look up the lyrics for Kenny Rogers's "Lucille" to see what I stumbled through.

I finally got permission to leave London on Friday, May 11. The system no longer failed.

I avoided driving as much as possible but managed to have a rear-end collision with a British auto on my last day due to wet roads. The driver of the car I hit was very excited and spoke very fast in a strong British accent. He kept yelling something about my car hitting his "boot," but how was I supposed to know they called the car trunks "boots" in London?

The Rush to Take Flight

I learned something else about the British that day: They queue up in a proper line for everything. When I saw a big line forming at the ticket counter, I was curious about what was happening, so I walked straight to the front of the line past at least a hundred queued vacationers. I heard the ticket agent tell every passenger the same thing: Our Braniff Airways jet had an accident in Dallas, so the return flight was canceled[7]. They told us to go to the side door and catch the shuttle bus to Heathrow where we could find another flight.

I left in such a hurry to take a shuttle to Heathrow Airport to find a flight back to the States that I didn't bother trying to retrieve my checked luggage. At Heathrow, there were no other flights to D/FW[8], so I got on standby to Chicago O'Hare airport. Luckily, I made the flight and literally ran through customs at O'Hare, since I had no luggage, sprinting to the gates and getting on standby to Dallas. I made that flight also.

As I walked down the gate tarmac in D/FW, I saw my

---

7. The jet had a food service truck blow over on the wing because of high winds at the D/FW airport.
8. Sadly, on August 2, 1985, D/FW airport was the site of a tragic jet crash, Delta Flight 191. It crashed short of the runway during the landing approach in a severe thunderstorm due to a new weather phenomenon called wind shear. In 1996, Doppler radar was installed at only four airports to detect wind shear.

company president, Bill M., walking to his gate. He asked where I was headed. I said Austin but told him I had no flight reservation. He said to follow him, and I got on standby for his flight, a flight I also made. He graciously drove me to my apartment where I called security to let me in since my keys were in my luggage.

What a trip!

Later, all employees were banned from renting a car overseas. Braniff Airlines went bankrupt in 1982 and went belly-up in 1989[9].

QUESTIONING THE SYSTEM

Many people fail to realize that taking simple steps when solving problems is the best way to find big solutions. And it's something that anyone can do.

Whether you're a frequent caller to the help desk or create computers (and everything in between), the biggest solutions to your problems come from starting small and moving up. As you saw in this story, sometimes the best solution is just to give the computer (or your brain) a jolt.

---

9. Braniff became one of the best-recognized airlines in existence due to its pioneering achievements. It was among the first to make nonstop flights from Tokyo to Dallas in 1966 and became the headliner for connecting distant parts of the world. Unfortunately, the retirement of one of its founders in 1980 set it on a downhill course, and economic problems made it shut down permanently a few years later. Look into Braniff Airlines if you're interested. The history is quite interesting.

CHAPTER FIVE

WHEN ARE YOU GOING TO GET THE DAMNED THING FIXED?

When I first entered the help desk, I worked in a small office. The administrative assistant sat at the center, and everyone could see everyone else throughout the office. I got a clear vision of what it was like to answer calls from demanding people.

If there was a problem no one could fix on the phone, the problem was escalated to management. I remember multiple occasions when the customer's escalated call was very hostile. It's a problem most people in the industry have to face at some point. These hostile people exist, and you have to be prepared for what they dish out.

FACING THE STORM

Some customers become angry at an entire company when something doesn't work right. And some customers have a lot of power and are not afraid to use it.

Some help desk professionals crumble under the pressure of constantly answering the phone, concentrating on new problems, or falling into a rut of working on the same problems repeatedly.

Working on a phone support team means you do not get to pick your daily assignments; the assignments pick you. Many veterans liken it to post-traumatic stress disorder (PTSD)[1].

Sometimes a company screws up or is unfairly blamed for someone else's problem (rarely is it a design problem). Sometimes it's a manufacturing problem. Sometimes the customer is at fault. Sometimes it's a third party's fault. And sometimes it is a combination of problems. It doesn't really matter; the customer's business is at stake, and he or she is going to do everything in his power to get it fixed.

And he or she doesn't care about who he or she must run over to do it.

All it takes is for an executive of a global company to call the president of your company and threaten to kick the equipment out on the street and then all hell breaks loose. There are a lot of reputations at stake. Here are stories about two different types of problems I had to solve back-to-back. I dare anyone to diagnose these problems via a help desk or using an AI help desk.

VIVA LA FRANCE!

On one such occasion, I flew to Paris on short notice. Once again, I didn't know what situation I was walking into. The president of my company just told my upper management to send their best person over to get their equipment fixed.

I arrived at Charles de Gaulle International Airport on a Sunday afternoon. Someone was waiting for me, holding a sign with my name. He greeted me by saying, "Here's your key to your rental car. Follow me, and let's go."

---

1. It reminds me of the scene in the movie "The Office" where the person was answering back-to-back calls and saying the same thing over and over, causing a mental breakdown.

I said, "Wait, let's talk about this. And I need to go to the restroom."

He said, "No, we have to go now."

Two hours later, we pull into the parking lot of a hotel. My bladder was full, and I suspect my eyes painfully projected my discomfort. He pointed to the building next door and said, "There is the customer site. Be there at 8 am. There is your hotel. Goodbye."

I said, "Wait, where can I get food? I'm hungry." He pointed to a shopping mall across the street and drove away.

A Play on Language

The name of the mall was the Parley II (pronounced Par-lay-doo) and was one of the biggest malls in France. I checked into the hotel. I was starving. All I had were American Express traveler's checks. We didn't have credit cards back in 1979[2]. The hotel had vending machines, but I didn't want vending food. So, I walked over to the mall and crossed a major highway with no pedestrian walkway.

All the restaurants were closed because it was late on a Sunday evening, all except one sandwich shop. I didn't read or speak French, and the menu was only in French. I tried to speak to the worker in English, but that was hopeless. I was walking out disgusted and frustrated when I heard someone behind me speak to me. There was a table with four young women. One of them tried to get my attention, but I couldn't understand her. I went over and told her I didn't speak French. Then she pointed at my digital wristwatch[3] and said in English, "What time is it?" I told her the time, she thanked me, and I turned around and walked to

---

2. Later, companies issued American Express Business credit cards to travelers for travel expenses.
3. Texas Instruments introduced the first under-$20 LED digital watch in 1976.

the door, but then it occurred to me like a slap to the face: she could translate the menu!

I went back and she said her English was not very good, so I asked her "Sprechen Sie Deutsch?" I had recently been to Germany for sixteen days, had taken a language course, and knew a few German dishes. But she said no. Then I asked her "Habla Espanol?" She said "Si." She was born in Mexico. She translated the menu from French to Spanish, and I ordered a ham sandwich with pomme frites.

Wow! That was an interesting start to my trip.

The French Diagnosis

I showed up at the customer site the next morning at 8 am. It was the regional headquarters of a leading global transportation company, and they had installed three full racks of our computers connected in a large room with other brands of computers. The other computers were much older and were used to download data from the company offices daily and transfer it to our computers using large reels of 9-track magnetic tape.

I noticed the manager's office was a glass-enclosed room in the corner on the second floor. Someone waved and motioned for me to come upstairs. I went up. He handed me the phone and said, "It is for you."

The call was from London, the European general manager of the company. I will never forget his next words: "We hate your company! We hate your computer! We hate you, and when are you going to get the damned thing fixed!?"

That was the most hostile situation I had ever experienced. I needed a miracle to rescue this one.

I don't remember my exact words, but I put myself in an unfavorable negotiating position. This guy definitely had the upper hand, and he was playing a very serious game. I think I said that I would do my best. He said something like I had until Friday, or they were kicking the computer out on the street.

I found an operator that spoke English, and he showed me the first problem. The main computer would shut down by itself during heavy workloads. I had a theory that it was a power supply, but I had no tools or equipment. I was all alone and had no local support, so I called the president of my company in Dallas and asked for help. An oscilloscope, some schematics, and an extender board (so I could probe inside the computer) arrived on Wednesday. I had a short time to fix it.

Our system was designed with modular 120-watt power supplies mounted on the backplane with socketed connectors. It was designed to support up to four power supply modules, each providing a maximum amount of power on a common voltage plane. Most installations only needed one or two power supply modules. This system needed four because it was so full of cards and memory. Each power supply module was about eight inches square, with heavy iron magnetic transformers and large bulk filter capacitors. They weighed about six pounds each.

I theorized that the power supply was sensing an overcurrent condition and shutting down to prevent physical damage. I knew if one of the supplies tried to supply more than its share of the current, it could throw an overcurrent alert and shut down the entire system.

I measured the voltage on the supplies one at a time and traced the problem to an imbalance in the setting of the 5-volt regulator on the power supplies. Luckily, I was familiar with the design and the adjustment to the voltage regulator. I fabricated a long-insulated screwdriver and adjusted the potentiometer (a variable resistor connected to a discrete op-amp-based circuit) while measuring the voltage on the oscilloscope and set the voltage of each supply under load to the same voltage of 5.10V +/- 5mV. This was a factory problem. The factory tolerance was 25 mV

66 CHAPTER FIVE

(millivolts) during the final test, but it needed to be 5mV to avoid the overcurrent imbalance issue[4].

The next issue involved tape reading errors. While I waited for the oscilloscope, I traced the problem to excessive channel skew on the 9-track 1600 bits-per-inch (BPI) phase-encoded (PE) magnetic tapes created on another computer. Our tape drive could read and write correctly, but the tapes written on one of the other computers would occasionally get errors when data was transferred on tape from the other computer. As it turned out, the other computer was designed to allow more tape channel skew during recording than our controller was designed to handle, but it was marginal. Our controller had automatic retries built in. If a record got a read error, it would re-read it many times before giving up.

I saw the tape moving back and forth and knew what was happening. I had taught a class on this[5], so I understood the decoder circuit. I called John Blaglia[6], and we came up with a firmware change over the phone. The tape controller had a 16-bit microprocessor and three asynchronous state machines. He fantastically documented the design and the firmware; he was the absolute best if you ask me. We transmitted the firmware fix electronically and got a programmable read-only memory (PROM) burner from the France office. I burned the PROMs and installed them, which fixed the second problem. Yes, we had those in stock and available. Thank goodness.

The third problem was the excessive use of the old magnetic tape reels. These things get dirty over time, wear out, and lose

---

4. I really enjoyed spending time in the power supply lab at the factory. I learned a lot from the design team.
5. I had studied it and taught classes on it in Singapore.
6. John was born in Romania. He escaped through the Iron Curtain to come to America. He was the genius that designed our tape controllers.

some of their magnetic properties, causing errors. The solution was a quick fix: replacement.

Just before departing the Robert Mueller Airport in downtown Austin, I noticed a sign that announced the opening of an international customs office on a certain date in two weeks. Later, I needed the French office to send me a magnetic tape reel with an error on it for analysis. I told them to ship it "Hold at Austin Robert Mueller U.S. Customs office." I was the first person to receive a package at the new customs office on the morning of the opening[7]. I got my picture in the newspaper.

BOOMERANG NAK

When I got back to the hotel in France, there was an urgent message from my boss. He said I needed to go to Birmingham, England to work on a networking issue. The next available flight was Sunday morning, so off I went again.

The state-of-the-art mainframe communications was a dedicated leased telephone line running at 56K baud, full duplex. Until that time, only half-duplex communications were supported by our high-speed networking equipment, meaning that only one side could transmit at a time because the clock was synchronous. This was before ethernet[8].

The customer had leased a 56K baud line from British Telecom (BT). We were running in full-duplex mode but occasionally got a communications error or negative acknowledg-

---

7. Prior to that, when I needed something shipped from overseas, it had to go through Houston, and it was so slow.
8. ARPAnet was the first wide-area packet-switched networking technology invented in 1969 by the US Department of Defense. Bob Metcalfe and David Boggs wrote the first published paper on Ethernet technology in 1976, and the Institute of Electrical and Electronics Engineers (IEEE) adopted it as the 802.3 standard on June 23, 1983, and paved the way for the modern Internet IBM introduced Token-Ring proprietary Local Area Network technology in 1984 but was more expensive to implement than Ethernet.

(NAKs or NACKs) on the data transmission from the remote site. I called Herman Dierks, one of our networking experts, and asked for his help to characterize the problem. I was told how to run diagnostics to test the problem, and we found that it occurred if the host sent data first and the client sent data before the host finished. I hooked up a high-speed scope and captured what looked like a phase shift in the clock when the line turned around, switching from sending data from one side to the other[9].

It was supposed to keep running the clock synchronized to the host clock. The cable connecting the computer to the modem used digital signals, and I connected them to a scope to make sense of them. The signal on the phone line was analog and implemented a technology called quadrature amplitude modulation (QAM) so a clock and two data channels could share the same wire simultaneously.

A dedicated leased telephone line is a pair of twisted copper wires. It's sufficient for short connections, but this one was over a mile away from the host. As a solution, BT added some repeaters between the host and the client to keep the signal strong enough. At the time, BT had a problem with some of their repeaters and upgraded to fix the problem[10].

We made some calls and got a BT engineer to show up on-site. We showed him the problem, and he acknowledged the issue. However, it took an act of Congress for them to get someone out,

---

9. At the time, test points were designed in printed circuit boards and electronic assemblies. Test points were specific spots where probes could be attached and used to help engineers test electronic signals. It's vital to make sure the system functions properly. We attached a scope to the test point, which showed the clock voltage in waveform. We looked at the amplitude, frequency, noise, and other properties to test the performance, test the strength of the signal, and fix problems within the circuit. Now the process is much more streamlined. New instruments can detect problems faster and make sure that the signals are correct.

10. Older repeaters were more affected by the environment. Adding too many repeaters meant that the signal wasn't very strong, so the signal couldn't make it through to provide reliable communication.

trace the problem to the specific repeater, and replace it with the upgraded one[11].

In the meantime, we could work around it by disabling full-duplex mode temporarily.

A CUSTOMER-FIRST APPROACH

Not every problem has an easy solution. Sometimes it's caused by the customer, and sometimes it's an internal problem. But ultimately, that doesn't matter. All that matters is how the customer feels. More often than not, that's the obstacle that you need to overcome.

Casting blame not only isn't helpful, but it also creates a barrier between yourself and the customer. All the customer wants to know is that the problem is fixed. If you spend too much time debating on who caused the problem, you're going to lose them. Even angry customers can change their minds if you approach the problem with the right attitude.

---

11. Adding too many variables in any system can lead to some serious problems. And, if you can't identify which of the variables is causing the problems, it can take a very long time to fix. You'd need to analyze every repeater individually to make sure you didn't miss something.

CHAPTER SIX
WHO'S THE BOSS?

THERE ARE SO MANY SMALL, ALMOST IMPERCEPTIBLE things in nature that can cause serious problems. What's the lesson here? The laws of nature are the boss. Here are nine true stories about how natural forces interfered with electronic systems.

CAPTAIN ZAP

If a tree falls in the forest but no one hears it, does it make a sound? If a stack of printed paper builds up a big, invisible static charge, where does the voltage and current go when it suddenly discharges?

Before I joined the help desk, I saw the effects of static charge firsthand. Our computers were popular, and I was happy to see them installed around the office with printers. The printers had to be physically located close to the main computer and were directly connected using a short industry-standard 25-pin RS-232 serial printer cable. These were much less expensive than the previous generation 36-pin parallel port cables. And they came with an optional metal stand and wire basket.

But we had a problem when the printer was attached: the computer stopped randomly. While I have told crazy stories of my exploits across the world, surprisingly, this problem happened in our own office. I heard it described in meetings.

After the problem had been going on for a long time, I sat down for coffee with one of the techs, and he described the problem to me. I was in the manufacturing test unit at the time, and no one consulted with me to solve the problem. The tech pointed out a machine that failed often, and it even failed as we walked by. I diagnosed the computer and concluded that it was in the normal state after a master reset. No one was able to figure out how it got there. It ran fine until someone printed a big job: dozens of sheets of fan-fold paper. I could hear the *zap*s when the static electricity was discharged.

I identified the problem as the static discharge of the paper to the metal paper basket. As the paper moved over the plastic exit slot of the printer, the friction generated a static charge, and it collected on the paper until it built up enough to discharge to the closest thing it could find, which was the metal basket. They had tried grounding the basket with a heavy green wire, but it still failed.

I had an idea.

I knew the master reset signal was a very long copper trace, the longest one on the backplane board where all the CPU and peripherals were plugged in, and it ran up and down the outside of the board in the shape of a large letter U. I knew electromagnetic energy could resonate in a long copper wire like an antenna and induce a voltage. Even though the circuits that received the reset signal had a glitch filter, it still got through. I knew a static discharge was like a miniature radio transmitter with a broad spectrum of electromagnetic energy. I knew that the backplane of the computer chassis had an unpopulated filter capacitor component on the master reset signal, and it was removed to reduce cost because it was thought to have no use.

I had experience testing that board. The power supply research lab had some 1000pf 600V ceramic capacitors that fit in the holes. I grabbed one and modified the board with a soldering iron. Lo and behold, the system never failed again.

That was not the first time I had to come up with a product change, so I contacted the manufacturing team, and they said I had to submit an engineering change order (ECO) form with the part number to add to the bill of materials (BOM).

The manufacturing team rejected the part number I gave because it was "too expensive, over-rated for the application, and not available in large quantities." So, they substituted another part with only a 25V rating instead of the 600V rating. It seemed to work for a while, but they still saw problems after a few months. I was called in as a consultant, and we replaced the cap; it started working again but failed again a few days later. I told them to use a higher voltage rating, and it never failed again. The reset signal was a 5V signal, but a glitch from the static discharge induced a high voltage, damaging the substitute capacitor.

Not long after that, our company expanded its email service. The email server was a mainframe, and email addresses were limited to a maximum of four characters. My first name had four characters, but it was already taken, so I took the email address "ZAP."

THUNDER!

Sometime after my stint at the help desk, our company licensed the rights to manufacture a state-of-the-art technology device. We had a clean room built at one of our office buildings, but there was a problem with yield. The team had done an analysis and ruled out problems with the clean room. I was called in as a consultant and went down for an inspection. I was shown engineering data that isolated the problem to an electrical error on one of thousands of digital control channel recordings[1]. It was a step in manufacturing that took a long time, but no one found a cause for the problem, and it didn't happen every day. Sometimes they would go for weeks without any failures.

The clean room had a special table built for some of the manufacturing steps, including recording digital control channels. In short, it was constructed to isolate the floor of the table from the rest of the building because vibration had to be minimized. The floor for the table was fastened to the bedrock of the ground beneath the building.

I collected the failure data and finally decided to check the correlation to the weather. Lo and behold, the drop in yield was directly correlated to rainstorms. When the ground was very wet, low-frequency vibrations from the nearby major roadway or thunder coupled into the bedrock and shook the table. I borrowed an extra sensitive vibration analyzer and proved the table was vibrating beyond the allowed tolerances. There were large potholes in the roadway, and sometimes big, heavy trucks went by at high speed and vibrated the ground so hard the table shook. It was so small that the workers didn't notice. This was proven, and the solution was to check for the issue caused by the excessive vibration and repeat recording of the control channels. That fixed the yield issue.

CHILL!

Have you ever gone outside after a thunderstorm and were amazed at how fresh the air smelled? Or have you noticed when

---

1. There was a new technology developed at the time to improve the efficiency of disk drives. This new tech used a pivot instead of a motor to move the heads linearly across the disk surface. The heads of the motor attached to an arm assembly that pivoted around a fixed point and swung over the platters. The new tech had more speed, was more compact, and was more durable than the previous disk drive tech. But, because it was new, it was extremely sensitive.

the outside air is dry, you get a little zap when sliding across a floor in polyester, your socks, or your chair? Ions are the cause. Lightning from the thunderstorm increases the negative ions in the air. Normally the air outside has a relatively balanced number of negatively and positively charged ions. It's measured in ions per cubic centimeter. Moisture in the air drains excess ions from objects.

We had a component with moving parts that had a seasonally high failure rate. I was assigned the task of determining the cause and a solution. I analyzed two years' service history data from all over the USA and directly correlated the failures to a sudden and large reduction in outside temperature: a.k.a. a cold front hit the location.

I couldn't reproduce the failure in a walk-in temperature chamber. Luckily, we had a research lab in another town, and I was able to borrow an ion density meter. I verified the walk-in chamber, which had thick metal walls, had zero positive and negative ions. I built an airtight box using plastic and used an industrial-sized desiccant to reduce moisture from the air, thus reducing the relative humidity. I verified the air in the chamber had the same number of ions as normal air using the ion density meter. When a cold front comes in, it brings dry air, making the relative humidity drop significantly. As the humidity in the box dropped slowly over six days of testing, the static charge on a Kapton™ cable increased gradually.

When it finally hit 600V as measured by my static meter, it started arcing, which I confirmed on an oscilloscope. Even a grounded conductor in a static field will polarize and generate a static discharge under some conditions. In our case, the gap between the conductor in the cable and a metal piece was about 0.008 inches. The dielectric strength of air is about 75,000 volts per inch or 75 volts per 0.001 inch. I had a theory it would take a static charge of about 600V to arc.

And I proved it.

The failures occurred when the air got very dry, and the static charge built up more rapidly on this cable because the material was highly non-conductive. Humid air drained the charge before it was large enough to jump the gap. The solution was to increase the gap and apply an insulator on the conductor. My manager called Bravo-Sierra, but that was the cause of the issue. It took me a year to figure this one out.

I also found microscopic evidence of tiny pits from the arcing on failure analysis and found a teardrop-shaped magnetic erasure pattern around the pit, which I could see using a polarization filter on the microscope. The pits ranged from 75 to 150 microinches in diameter, and the recording track was about 250-300 microinches wide. The erasure decreased the amplitude of the signal between 50% and 90%, depending on the position of the pit. I had the pits analyzed by a scanning electron microscope. I did another experiment to prove that the voltage correlated. I used a static generator to create pits at different voltages and found that 600V of static would create a pit of about 125 microinches.

LIGHTS OUT!

Before the events of "Chill!", I wasn't available to travel, so Adolf, one of our disk controller design engineers, volunteered to go to a power plant customer site in Ohio to debug a problem. He called me while he was on the customer site and described the problem. It failed frequently, and I told him to turn off the lights, climb underneath the disk drive, and check if he saw any static discharge. To his surprise, while he was underneath the Trident Disk drive, he saw bright flashes when the spindle discharged static to the index sensor. I could hear the static discharge on the landline phone as a zapping noise.

The power plant was coal-fired, and the dust from the exhaust was non-conductive. The computer was installed in a remote location in a utility building near the coal plant and was very dusty. The spindle spun using a rubber belt connected to an electric motor. The belt was constructed with threads of conductive carbon fiber to help remove static charges from the spindle. However, the dust collected around the surface between the belt and the spindle and built up a large static charge on the belt. The static charge jumped the gap to the bracket that held the index sensor. When that happened, the electrostatic discharge caused an index error which caused the disk drive to reset.

We solved the problem by designing an anti-static drive pulley. The standard drive pulley had a non-conductive surface. The new pulley had a solid metal exterior ring that the belt contacted. This solved the problem.

SOS!

Speaking of static, control of static electricity during the electronic assembly manufacturing process was an innovation during the early part of the information age. I became a member of the IEEE because they developed standards for testing electronic equipment sensitivity to electrical overstress/electrical static discharge (EOS/ESD). I read as many published papers as I could on the subject and attended symposiums in person to learn as much as I could and speak to other interested people.

I learned that semiconductor manufacturing facilities were installing electronic ionizers in clean rooms to control static charges. The ionizers generated a high concentration of negative ions to attempt to balance the ions in the air. Unfortunately, electronic ionizers also generated ozone, which could deteriorate rubber and plastic material and slough off particles from the tungsten electrodes inside the ionizer. Particles in a clean room are bad news for semiconductors.

I learned that there were at least four ways static electricity could be dangerous to electronics.

- When static charge touches an electronic component

The most obvious is when a person gets a static charge and touches the electronic component. Even if the component is not powered on, the static discharge could damage it. Persons should wear wrist straps or leg straps to ground themselves to prevent static charge and discharge. Static discharge to a circuit pin causes extremely rapid heating inside the device resulting in thermal damage due to overheating, not electrical failure.

The threshold of human sensation of a static discharge varies from person to person but is typically thought of to be around 2000V. Some very sensitive electronic devices are damaged with as little as 300V. A person can't feel static discharges that small. This is one of the reasons there are warning labels on consumer electronic enclosures. Service should be performed by authorized technicians only.

- When an unprotected component has an electrostatic field around it

If an unprotected sensitive component or assembly is carried by a person or object that has an electrostatic field around it, the field could induce a polarized voltage inside the electronic circuits causing the tiny circuits to become stressed by the static field, inducing a current, and thus causing thermal, not electrical, damage. Sensitive components and assemblies should only be transported in protective containers to static charges.

There are different levels of sensitive components identified by a label on component shipping containers. Employees should be trained on the identification of these levels and what they mean.

- When static charge clings to devices

Devices, such as equipment, furniture, printer paper, etc., can get a static charge on them. If they discharge to something, the electromagnetic energy emitted could radiate to sensitive components causing them to be upset or damaged. The rise-time and amplitude of charged devices are more damaging than charged persons.

- When machines generate their own static charge

As explained in the stories above, machines can generate their own static charges and discharge, causing physical damage[2].

There's a lot of ignorance about static. Many people don't realize how much of an effect static has on electronics, and it can lead to major problems. Before setting up new electronics, check electrical instruments for static.

BEING TENSE IS BETTER!

In my early troubleshooting days, we had an innovative high-speed impact line or drum printer made by a third party. Some of our customers needed to print on multi-part continuously fed paper and needed up to 600 lines per minute print speed. It was very expensive, loud, and heavy, and it was used by some of our most powerful customers. It helped us compete with more expensive computers made by our competitors. Because it was so loud, it needed to be placed in a separate room but still close to the computer cabinet.

This printer had a row of hammers that would strike the ribbon and impact the paper with the designated character. All the hammers fired at the same time. The hammer assembly then shifted back and forth and hammered the other characters. The hammer assembly was called the shuttle, and when it was moving, we called it shuttling. If the printer was idle, the shuttle would

---

2. Search "CDM, HBM static" for more information.

stop shuttling gradually as it was mounted on springs. When data needed to be printed, it would shuttle up or start shuttling[3].

Behind the paper impact point was a heavy solid stainless-steel cylinder called the platen. The platen was adjustable for different thicknesses of paper. The paper was fan-folded and continuously fed. The sides of the paper had holes, and the printer had sprockets or tractors that fit in the holes, and a precision motor turned the tractor gears to advance the paper in precise amounts. The combination of the tractors, the platen, the weight of the paper, and friction kept tension on the paper. The tension was important to keep the paper from shifting so characters printed on the paper maintained a constant line spacing.

The most common type of paper was that green pin-striped zebra multi-part paper you may have seen in old movies such as *War Games*.

On our systems, when the system started printing, high-priority tasks could steal processing time, causing the low-priority print tasks to stall. When the printer's internal control logic detected a gap in incoming print data, it went into a low power mode, which removed power from the spinning hammer drum. The vibration of motors starting and stopping the spinning print hammer drum caused the continuous feed paper to shift slightly unless friction between the paper and the platen maintained the relative paper position for the next line to print.

I interviewed the owner of the new platen via phone call. His perception of quality was related to the appearance of the sparkle on the surface of the platen, and his company polished the platen to a brilliant shine. This had the disadvantage of low friction to the paper movement. The owner spoke very proudly of his firm's ability to manufacture a shiny platen product, and, in his opinion, it was an improvement over the existing product at a lower cost. The original platen manufactured in-house had a dull surface that

---

3. Search "line printers" for more information.

provided a perfect amount of friction between the paper and the platen to prevent line-spacing anomalies.

What they didn't know was the dull surface on the original platen increased friction between the paper and the platen, and the friction was a critical design feature that helped guarantee the line spacing between lines when the spinning hammer drum motors were stopped and restarted.

The owner of the cost-reduced platen was embarrassed, and his feelings were hurt when I explained that the shiny surface on the platen he manufactured caused customer complaints in the field because they didn't meet the friction requirements. The specifications for the friction were not included in the documents sent to him by the purchasing department.

I asked the owner to send me samples of improved platens with a dull surface for testing. I received the new platens and tested them. I verified the friction met the line-spacing requirements under extreme stop/start conditions, informed HQ of the needed change, and requested a recall notice. We stocked new platens with the fix and sent out notices to our customers of the recall and repaired printers under warranty.

ISLAND ENCOUNTERS OF THE CIRCUIT KIND

In the early 90s, our company strived to innovate advanced 486 processors (CPU) to compete in a rapidly changing consumer PC market dominated by other companies. We introduced the industry's first write-back cache 486 processor, which enabled a new performance feature to perform burst writes of 64-byte blocks to memory instead of individual write-through 8-byte writes.

In the earlier CPUs, the cache was used to store read data or writes to an address already contained in the cache but writes also were sent to RAM one 8-byte write at a time. Cache memory consisted of high-speed static RAM devices. Cache memory is high-power and expensive, therefore, the amount of cache memory in the CPU is limited. Write and read to RAM channel command ordering is critical and overhead was expensive in the timing budget, so the RAM channel stalled to allow the write commands to complete before processing more READ commands. Write-back cache memory policy allowed the write commands to update cache data if it already had a matching address and set the status of the cache location to the MODI-FIED cache state. Later, when the cache location needed to be replaced, the modified cache state forced the entire cache line of 64 bytes to be written in a burst write command, thus reducing the overall amount of memory channel stalls caused by streams of individual write commands. If the cache line had not been modified since filled or read from RAM, the cache location could be replaced by a different line without a write-back.

We had a potential partner in the top ten of the consumer desktop PC industry testing production samples of our new chips in their existing systems designed for one of the other companies' CPUs. The Northbridge chip was from the competing company which connected the CPU to the cache memory and the RAM. It was crucial to win this business because the other top ten PC makers could use our processors to compete if we could break into the top ten supply chain.

During their qualifying quality testing, they discovered that, after 72 hours in a thermal chamber at high operating temperature, our processor experienced memory data corruption. They asked for our help in diagnosing the root cause. We couldn't reproduce the problem in my lab when we connected a thermal head to heat the CPU package, so I suspected the root cause was either in the Northbridge chip or the printed wiring board (PWB).

The partner insisted we send an expert to help them resolve the problem. Although their HQ was in the USA, the design, manufacturing, and testing center was in Taiwan.

I selected one of my junior engineers, Huan L., and sent him on his way while I stayed and worked on reproducing the failure and analyzing the error.

I fabricated a make-shift thermal chamber to heat a sample of their motherboard using a 100-watt lamp from my home garage and was able to reproduce the problem. I monitored the CPU interface to the Northbridge with a DAS9000 protocol analyzer. I triggered a compare error and confirmed the read data didn't match the write data when:

- the pattern of data was a burst-write, and
- the sequence of data patterns included worst-case ones and zero switching.

Analysis of the layers on the printed circuit board indicated what I called a Swiss-cheese power island effect on the power layers. Based on my analysis, the instantaneous current flowing during signal switching during the burst-write command caused the input circuits to sample the input as a 1 instead of a 0 under certain conditions that only occurred because our CPU was able to transfer more back-to-back data during burst write operations.

I analyzed the power routing and ground copper in the PWB layout of the Northbridge power and ground solder balls and predicted the problem was caused by a transient voltage drop due to simultaneous signal switching caused by high impedance across the power plane copper conductors because the through-holes in the plane were too numerous, starving the power plane of current. At 2 am, I documented my findings and faxed them to the Taiwan office with instructions to give those details to Huan when he arrived in a few hours. We modified the printed circuit board layout in a meeting with their designers and resolved the issue.

Because we solved the problem and the PC makers started shipping systems with our 486 chips at a lower cost, we won designs from eight of the other top ten PC makers in the world in a short time.

READY, SET, WAIT FOR IT!

Most of this book was about my personal problem-solving experience to help readers understand how things work. As part of any good problem-solver student's habits, you should seek knowledge about other computer problems, not just your own. Learn about as many different types of system failures as possible to help quickly resolve or avoid new problems.

This true story caught my attention because the issue parallels some of my experience with not just electronics, but general science and physics also. It was kept a secret until after the end of the Cold War.

According to reports, in September 1983, the Cold War between the U.S.S.R. and the United States of America was dangerously close to a thermonuclear war. Both sides were prepared to launch counterattacks on a hair-trigger if incoming missiles were detected. The U.S.S.R. "OKO" (meaning "EYE") satellite infrared sensor readings were monitored by a new computer located in the Serpukhov-15 bunker. The U.S.S.R. installed the computer in 1982 to sound an alarm when it detected a missile launch from the U.S.A. toward Russia so a counterattack could be launched before the missiles reached their targets. A team of algorithm specialists took data from the computer and manually validated computer missile alerts to prevent the counterattack if needed.

According to the details provided by KGB agents, the satellite's infrared sensors were fooled at about midnight local Russia time on September 25 by a rare combination of sunlight from an equinox sun reflecting off high-altitude clouds and the timing of the satellite's orbit. The computer logged five missile launches from the Western U.S.A. a few minutes apart. The distance between the missile launch site and the Russian ground radar range meant minutes could pass until the missiles were close enough to be confirmed by ground radar. The Russian missile defense protocol dictated an immediate counterattack without ground radar confirmation.

Based on what I have learned about this incident online, I have a theory about the glitch: the computer flaw was missing critical program functions to make a distinction between infrared readings of a real missile engine exhaust plume and sunlight reflecting off high-altitude clouds. I suspect it was only programmed to detect a high-intensity infrared object moving from the U.S.A. toward Russia. I think sunlight, through water vapor in the clouds, refracted the light into the infrared frequency band used by the satellite to identify engine exhaust plumes of a missile launch. Due to the earth's rotation, the infrared signature from the clouds appeared to move toward Russia's coastline, which matched a potential missile trajectory. Cameras mounted on satellites were also available to confirm or deny missile launches visually, and reports say confirmations were hampered by the moving edge of the brightness of the morning sun over North America.

Thankfully, the Russian officer on duty at the bunker in charge of launching the counterattack suspected a computer malfunction caused the first false alarm and waited to launch a nuclear counterattack until ground radar confirmed or denied an incoming missile, even though superior officers pressured the officer to retaliate immediately for the missile attack reported by the computer. As four more missile launch alarms occurred back-to-back, the officer struggled with his decision to continue waiting for ground confirmation.

A Danish filmmaker released a documentary film in 2015 titled *The Man Who Saved the World*, not to be confused with a 2012 film about the Cuban missile crisis of the same name. Spoiler alert: In the over two-hour award-winning documentary, the Russian officer, now over 70 years old, played himself and spoke of the computer glitch briefly in a very subtle way. The highly acclaimed film also briefly hinted at his primary reason for not trusting the computer in a roundabout way: if the U.S.A. launched a preemptive nuclear strike, common sense clearly suggested that the computer should have detected a lot more than five missiles. He said no one ever determined the real reason for the five back-to-back false alarms.

THE BIG FLOP

Each day at the help desk has the potential to learn something new. Some of our customers requested we add support for a new inexpensive portable storage medium called the 8-inch floppy disk. I'd read about it, including the design specifications, but during pre-production testing, many read errors occurred[4].

The disk was a thin, flexible 8-inch round vinyl-like material with a thin magnetic coating adhering to the surface. It came inside a vinyl-like jacket sleeve with a large hole in the middle for the motor hub and two small holes, one for the index sensor and another for the write-protect sensor.

The data was written and read by flying magnets (Write/Read head) touching the disc at a calibrated distance from the index as the motor rotated the internal disc. The flying magnets were positioned by a precision stepping motor using a screw-drive mechanism to align to circular digital tracks. Paul calibrated the stepping motor position by monitoring the read data with an oscilloscope while reading a write-protected calibration disc which had known-good test patterns for calibrating the motor already written on the test disk. The only way to calibrate it was to flip the

---

4. The development lab was located near Aggieland in Hearne Texas. The EET responsible for analyzing and fixing the issue was Paul H. I was told to travel and help Paul figure out the problem.

drive up on its rear to access the test points with the scope probe while using a diagnostic to read data from each of the circular tracks. The scope probe test points were only accessible from the bottom of the disk drive. Flipping it upside down or onto the side was impossible because the power and control cables were connected at the rear.

The drive chassis was designed for a tabletop or mounted in a computer rack and could contain up to two drives in one chassis.

Paul analyzed some of the failing systems. They failed when running random track seek + write/seek + read diagnostic. Some gave inconsistent error rates. Paul checked calibration, and calibration was within specification. Paul demonstrated the calibration process to me by unscrewing the drive from the chassis, flipping it on its rear, inserting the calibration disc and scope probe, then reading the data and measuring the amplitude of the read signals. Then he detached the scope, flipped the drive back down to a flat horizontal position, replaced the calibration disk with a writable blank disk, then ran the test and counted the errors.

I suggested to Paul that he run the random write/read test with the drive flipped on the rear. Lo and behold, it stopped failing. The weight of the write/read heads and the screw drive mechanism on the stepper motor, while it was flipped on the rear edge, was different than lying flat. The difference in weight caused the stepping motor to position the heads differently when flat, causing intermittent read errors. The solution was simple; redesign the chassis with an access panel to allow calibration of the motor in the normal flat operating position. Scope test points should have been accessible in the normal operating position.

The first 8-inch floppy disc used single-sided single-density (SSSD) data format. The formatted capacity was approximately 80KB. Later, as the technology improved, Double-sided discs (DSSD) were introduced, and then soon after Double-density (DSDD) was introduced. Soon thereafter, the 5.25-inch floppy disc was introduced although the jacket was a rigid plastic case.

We still call them floppy discs. This almost made the 8-inch floppy obsolete. After the 3.5-inch floppy became a standard, the 8-inch floppy finally became obsolete.

After we root caused the floppy issue, Paul asked if I was related to his wife by marriage because he recognized my last name. He knew who my new bride was because his wife attended the annual family reunions also. Paul and I were distant relatives by marriage. Small world. We became friends and played golf together occasionally.

ROOTING OUT THE CAUSE

I recommend we always seek to determine the root cause(s) of system errors. There is a logical explanation to everything, and it's often not what we initially expect. It comes down to the bright people who are willing to find answers, even if it takes time and a lot of negative feedback.

CHAPTER SEVEN

THE DATABASE MONSTER

One of my tasks as a member of our corporate quality organization was to validate the monthly warranty service repair database. I didn't design the database, but I inherited the responsibility to use and validate it. Once I learned the process for implementing database changes, it made my life easier.

The field quality warranty report tabulated and calculated the replacement rate of components based on the part numbers and quantity entered on the service ticket by analyzing the service ticket database. I would download the raw service ticket history and manually read the comments the service repair person entered. Based on the serial number and part number of the system, the database knew how many of each component the system had shipped and, based on the total installed base of the components, calculated the failure rate by the number of times a component was replaced. If the same component was replaced on the same system multiple times, I had to determine if it was a repeat failure, incorrect diagnosis, or if a different part failed as there were multiple parts.

I found multiple instances of incorrect part numbers and serial numbers in the database. I could also see when the repair didn't really fix it and was counted as a failure, a.k.a. false failure[1]. It was important to estimate the failure rate to predict how many parts the service department needed to carry at the regional and local service inventory. We even recorded the tester number so, if a part failed, we could track it back to the individuals that tested the parts during manufacture.

I found numerous bugs in the database software, but the biggest problem occurred because the data entered wasn't validated. I traveled out to the field offices and talked to the folks entering the data. Usually, they called their dispatcher, the dispatcher collected the info by phone, and then entered it incompletely, but the repair person was blamed for the problem. Sometimes, the dispatcher didn't receive the information from the repair person and would be creative and just enter garbage. There were at least three reasons the information was entered manually incorrectly:

- The purpose of collecting the information accurately was not communicated clearly.
- Punishment for inaccurate data entry wasn't administered.
- Entering accurate information was time consuming.

Among other things, we eventually improved the system so the repair person could enter the information electronically[2].

THE DATABASE FLAW

---

1. False failures should not count against the product quality but should count toward field inventory requirements. Sometimes, the repair guy replaced the wrong part.
2. I was nominated by my peers for the prestigious "Quality Hall of Fame" inaugural award and was one of three first-time recipients. We were honored by a nice formal dinner including spouses with company executives plus received a nice plaque and bonus.

Automation can be a hero or a devil. There is an old saying: "Do you want it: Fast? Cheap? Good? Pick any 2." This applies to database design. Nobody has ever designed a database perfectly the first time in my honest opinion.

The database is only as good as the data entered into it. There are a lot of issues, and if you put garbage in, you'll get garbage out. This especially applies to call centers.

Let's say I want a database to capture all the call information and generate metrics to determine how my help desk pros are doing, measure customer satisfaction, measure product quality, or identify potential safety issues. Or all of the above. A lot of it depends on the type of product. I have spent a lot of time calling different help desks just to see how they handle calls.

- Financial companies: Banks, credit cards, mortgage companies, investment brokerages.
- Consumer products: Appliances, computers, phone service, cameras, internet service providers, cable providers.
- Government offices: Tax appraisal, city zoning and planning commission, city hall, state legislature.
- Personal services: Real estate agent, lawyer, psychiatrist, physician, tax preparation, home maintenance.

There is no one database solution for all these types of services and products.

In 2017, I received a tax appraisal for my single-occupant residence in Williamson County Texas, one of the fastest-growing counties in the U.S.A. My home was appraised for a much higher value than I thought it should be. I filed a protest, and the tax appraiser sent back a nice report of the comparable home sales within 90 days of the Jan 1st appraisal date. One of the recent home sales down the street was listed as a three-bedroom and

1500 square feet. I did some research and found a real estate listing for the same house as 1900 square feet and four bedrooms. The owner had converted the garage into another finished room and received a higher sales price, but the county database had not been updated and increased the average community price per square foot. Since the house was listed in the database with fewer square feet of living space, the average price per square foot of living space was much higher than in reality.

During my protest hearing, I showed the appraiser the information I had indicating their database was incorrect and got an instant reduction in the appraised value for my property, therefore, reducing my tax bill. None of my neighbors protested their tax appraisal so they all paid more taxes than was justified to the taxing entities.

ROOTS OF TECH

Remember, there are many categories of customers. Some are afraid of technology, (a.k.a. technophobes), and some are just plain ignorant. Stu had a saying: "We may be lost, but we are making good time." Ignorance is not insulting if it's genuine. Some disguise their ignorance by making up words or stories. There is no way a database will know the difference between truth and fiction by analyzing the words without their meaning[3].

Some words have roots in other words or languages. I invited a visitor from Deutschland (a.k.a. Germany) to our Texas ranch for Thanksgiving once. On the dirt road to the house was a live Texas armadillo he had never seen before. He used the German word "Panzeratte" to describe it, which literally translates to "Tank-rat," an accurate description of an armadillo.

Many words sound alike but are spelled differently and/or

---

3. Look up "fake word generator" for a few laughs. It's also important to note that AI engines have similar issues with bias in their algorithms.

THE DATABASE MONSTER 93

have completely different meanings. This makes verbal communication with customers difficult. I often prefer using online chat to communicate with my customers or if I need to contact technical support myself. I highly recommend providing an online chat option for your next help center project.

Sometimes a word needs to be spelled one letter at a time over the phone. Letter sounds can be misunderstood and cause database errors unless both persons know how to use Tango-Bravo phonetic alphabet codes, a.k.a. the Military Alphabet. This significantly decreases verbal transcription errors.

If the challenge is to extract useful data from the database which includes the words the customer and/or call-taker uses, it needs a way to validate the information.

CHAPTER EIGHT
IT SHOULDN'T FAIL LIKE THAT!

I WANT THE ELECTRONICS IN VEHICLES TO NEVER FAIL. If something does fail, I want it to fail predictably, be detected, and automatically enable a fail-safe or backup system. I want the same transportation reliability for my loving family and friends. Maybe I just don't trust electronic systems because my job for more than 47 years has been searching for answers to failures in electronics.

Unfortunately, electronic components are not perfect or fail-safe. The price of a product is highly dependent on the quality of the individual components used to build it. The Apollo 1 capsule fire and tragic deaths of the three astronauts would not have happened if a NASA contractor hadn't cut costs by using less costly material for the capsule[1].

Of course, this is hardly the only example of a failure to meet the right product specifications. If it's cheaper to make unreliable

---

1. It makes little sense to me why the government spends so much taxpayer money on high-reliability components for weapons when they just get destroyed anyway. I certainly want my spacecraft to never fail during use, but I don't really care if that missile doesn't blow up. I guess I am willing to pay for space-grade components on some things.

equipment, many manufacturers will gladly make the sacrifice. Some. Even go so far as to bake these unreliable elements directly into their products. A certain popular manufacturer today intentionally makes their products obsolete after years of updates to get you to buy more of their products.

The moral is that, unfortunately, money is king.

THE COSTS OF DEVELOPMENT

Product development in electronics consists of software and hardware plus mechanical components like fans, circuit boards, and chassis to perform a set of sub-tasks to a set of specifications. When combined with many other tasks, these individual parts constitute a finished product. Bringing new technology to the market many hours of research. During manufacturing and design, the product goes through a series of tests to ensure it meets specifications.

Building for Reliability

The notes taken when creating these products increase the chances of producing high-quality products. Products should be reliable, or at least have some predicted reliability to meet market perception. We expect higher quality for an expensive luxury car than an economy car even though they are both designed and built by the same manufacturer. We pay more for organic produce. There are different grades of components for different uses. In the order of least to most reliable are consumer grade, automotive grade, commercial grade, medical grade, aeronautic grade, military grade, and space grade.

Narrow down the reliability grade of your product before selling. Basing the reliability of your products on the bathtub curve[2],

---

2. The initial stage of the bathtub curve represents the early failure period, and

illustrating the failure rate of a product or system over its lifecycle, can help you analyze the pattern of failure. You can also use the Weibull analysis to help you narrow down failure rates[3]. Though these are some of the most common ways to predict failure, explore others to make your product as well-rounded as possible.

Build products with the costs of high-quality products in mind and save enough money in your budget for product testing. The truth is that there are thousands of ways for things to go wrong. It's impossible to account for all of them, but predicting as accurately as possible through testing is the best way to start.

So many companies now are looking for a quick buck and expect failures in their products. Things aren't as reliable as they used to be. After all, if a product isn't reliable, your customers can always sell and upgrade their products. But good quality with longevity should be the standard for electronic production, even if it comes at a higher cost.

Scripting the Way

Along the way, often at the last minute, someone decides to develop the help desk scripts with an educated guess on the type of questions or problems a customer may have with the product and a list of possible troubleshooting steps with suggested solutions.

If the help desk works properly, unanswered or unsolved issues escalate until the problem is resolved. From there, hope-

---

failure rates are high due to manufacturing defects, design inadequacies, and material weaknesses, among other early design flaws. After the initial failure period, the number of issues goes down and the product enters its most reliable part of its lifecycle. During the final phase, the product enters its wear-out failure period when it suffers from wear and tear, material degradation, and general cumulative damage from operation.
3. The Weibull analysis method involves collecting and plotting data and then estimating parameters. Once you analyze the most likely areas for failure, you can then predict future failures.

the scripts will be revised to become more efficient and thorough. In rare cases, the unresolved issues are the result of product design flaws, a manufacturing test escape, or just bad luck with an unreliable sub-component.

Many developers don't include copious amounts of notes associated with their creations. It's difficult to help someone with a product if there isn't a manual to help them through it. Including subtext within the code is essential to people on the front lines of the sales market. The people setting up these new systems are among your most valuable assets. The more they understand, the more information they can communicate to people working behind help desks.

The Technical Support Grade

Maybe technical support teams should also be given a grade. They are just as important as the product designers. The help center should be designed to meet the customer's expectations. Easy to say but hard to measure.

Technical support is often difficult, and there's a lot of turnover. But, if companies bake fun into their businesses, they can increase the responsiveness of their employees and lower the turnover rate. You'll see a vast increase in your company's technical support grade when team members regularly see recognition and have brainstorming sessions to come up with solutions. Focusing on your team's growth can significantly improve the work experience.

I would much rather work with teams that have smiles on their faces than serious faces or frowns. Working at some companies was fun because the people working there were fun and interesting, not because there was a corporate mandate that employees should enjoy coming to work.

Natural work groups form when they have the freedom to share ideas and management support to implement changes and recognition for individual contributions. I think this starts with the low-level managers. I had great first-level managers: Jerry W., Susie B., and Albert J. I received professional classroom training that allowed me to become an effective manager because I learned the importance of involving all individuals to ask for their input. Too often, only the loudest individuals get the attention in a meeting and make the meeting about them.

If people are too busy, overworked, and micromanaged, or they have significant input to give but never the opportunity to communicate, they will be unhappy; unhappy people, especially in the design environment, make mistakes and create bugs. If I respect my manager or team leader, I want to do a good job to make him or her like me, and, of course, to hopefully get a pay increase.

People need to feel their work is meaningful and be recognized for their contributions. I don't mind if my manager takes credit for the work of his or her team or individuals as long as he or she publicly recognizes the efforts of teams and individuals who put in the effort. Sometimes an individual makes personal sacrifices to finish a task and exerts effort far beyond expectations. These people are the superheroes of the industry and don't get enough recognition. Eventually, management, especially upper management who makes the annual budget decisions, takes this extra effort for granted, especially if the lower management doesn't highlight the sacrifices made by individuals to get the job done. This leads to an overestimation of the ability of the team on the next project[4].

MANAGEMENT OF HUMAN RESOURCES

---

[4]. On the other hand, when I was a newbie at another large three-initial corporation, my co-workers resented me for completing more work than them. They said I made them look bad.

Many leaders underestimate how many people they need to run their companies. Companies decide what percentage of the budget should be spent on customer technical support and help center teams before they even know the reliability, or the level of support needed for the product and its customers.

It's a significant investment to build a help center. How would you control costs? If you ask the design team management how many bugs their finished product will have, they will say zero. In reality, they have no idea what they didn't design correctly or the hidden bugs they didn't find. Product development is also a major investment.

If the development plan includes zero design bugs post-product launch, why does staff need a help desk or customer technical support? Someone has to make a decision when the product is ready to launch. Product development managers get bonuses for delivering their new product on time, not for reaching zero bugs in use.

Corporate executives get big bonuses from the board of directors when they meet product launch schedules. Customers ask for the new product to ship with no delays. There is tremendous pressure on the product release teams to get the product out the door. The product quality managers, if they exist, should get an equal vote on the readiness of the new product to ship to customers. In my opinion, traditional quality management only gives lip service to product quality. I think that should change. Managers and executives need to be held accountable for any quality or customer issues when the product fails to meet expectations[5]. You can take some risks if the failure causes a slight inconvenience, but if it calculates my bank statement incorrectly, I have to draw the line.

---

5. I am talking about financial incentives for quality instead of meeting delivery schedules.

Testing for Success

Product testing plays an important role in building a quality product. Tests should stress the sub-task at its lowest level and check for errors. But sometimes a sub-test is omitted to reduce test time and/or because there is an assumption that one of the higher-level tests will find the problem if it exists. There is usually a test plan based on a specification that lists all the types of possible failures. If one of the sub-tasks has an error or a "bug," it generates a specific visible error indicator. Sometimes the error is invisible (a.k.a. Silent Error), and these errors are the hardest types to find.

Sometimes, the error messages are humorous. Carl Wilson used to have a saying from his former oil field work at Shell Development Company back in the 60s. Stu Barrett wrote about adding that error message to a released product: "Yes, I first heard of the 'Shut'er down' phrase from Carl back in Commerce Park in Houston. I just coded it into our products. Even got a write-up in Byte and PC magazines." Stu used to refer to his fellow computer scientists fondly with the phrase, "We are on the 'foreskin' of technology!"

Mike Irrgang recalled that error message creating chaos on the help desk. "I recall that exact message: 'Shut her down Clancey, she's a-pumpin' mud.' It was a new release of the Distributed Network Operation System (DNOS) when I was the manager of the customer support hotline in the 80s. Suddenly everyone from around the world started calling us (HUNDREDS of calls) asking what it meant! We had to pull the release and fix the bug that triggered it!" When all the interrupt handlers got a fatal error, the computer would show that error message. This was not supposed to happen, but a bug triggered it on all the systems after a software upgrade. And of course, it was undocumented[6].

---

6. I highly recommend searching for the history of computer bugs and Grace Hopper, the first computer software programmer, for more information. She was

SEARCHING FOR RAM

How do you test the memory sub-system with a memory test? There are many types of failures that a memory sub-system can experience. Some of the failures are very common. But if the memory fails, how can you determine what failed? What if replacing the memory doesn't fix the memory error problem? Can a memory error be caused by a software problem[7]?

Random access memory (RAM) requires software to initialize it. In the 1970s, I worked for a firm that developed the first 16Kb RAM chip. It was state-of-the-art technology. Most of the previous chips were only capable of storing 1Kb or 4Kb of data. It took eight of the chips to store 1KB or 4KB. Increasing the capacity to 16KB decreases the number of chips (a.k.a. integrated circuits (ICs)) by four or sixteen to make a 16KB subsystem. In a large system, one of the RAM devices would predictably give an error at some time in its lifecycle; therefore, it was necessary to add a ninth chip to include the parity bit that was needed to detect RAM errors to make the failure visible. If a parity error occurs while running a program, the bus master that requested the RAM access would report the error[8].

Bus masters (BM) include disk controllers, CPUs, and network controllers. BMs have access rights to read and write RAM directly instead of going through a central bus interface

---

a captain in the U.S. Navy when I met her. She became an Admiral. Learn what a nanosecond is.

7. What is RAM? Search "history of random-access-memory" for more information. How do you design a computer to use RAM? Search "memory controller" for more information.

8. To ensure data integrity, some memory systems use parity checking, which detects mechanisms that can identify errors in data storage or during a data transfer. The bus master is the component that controls data transfers in the computer's bus, which connects different parts of the computer to hardware devices. When the bus master encounters a parity error, it means that the integrity of the data accessed is compromised.

and can generate interrupts to the controlling CPU. Every time the BM writes to RAM using parity error detection, it also writes the parity bit. When the info is read back, the memory checks if the parity of the data matches the parity stored when it was written. If a mismatch occurs, you get a parity error interrupt or exception vector, usually via a separate alert signal wire or message. Parity is ideal if it implements "ODD" parity to detect cases when all the bits are written as zeros incorrectly. If all nine bits are zero, a parity error is signaled. The parity bit must be a 1 to make ODD parity. In the RAM technology used at the time, if a RAM failed, the bit stored as logic 1 would fail to logic 0. It would rarely fail a 0 to a 1[9].

That's boring to many of you. 99% of the time, you call the help desk with a parity error and the trouble script suggests a solution: tell the customer to replace the RAM card or memory card. But what if, after replacing the card, the error persists? Replace the bus master that reported the error. Then, if that still fails, replace it again. And what if it still fails?

It isn't supposed to fail like that.

In most cases, the help desk scripts will just keep repeating the same repair step because most help desk professionals don't know any better. This drives customers insane, and some get very angry, sometimes violently outraged. Let's hope your customers don't go postal over unsatisfactory customer support[10].

---

9. Hexadecimal numbers included the letters A-F for 10 through 15, and someone thought it was a good idea to initialize all the memory with the pattern "DEAD" instead of all zeros. This came in handy when searching memory for patterns.

10. My internet service provider in 2019 had an annoying robo-help menu when selecting internet tech support; it repeated the modem-reboot troubleshooting step every time someone called, even if they had done that step before. It's very effective at making the customer hang up and hope the problem resolves itself. I guess that is one way to improve your call closure rate, artificially in my honest opinion.

THE DENMARK BUG

I was sent to Denmark to troubleshoot (a.k.a. "debug") a system problem where the restore of a backup disk crashed with a fatal disk parity error. It failed every time, even after replacing everything twice. The customer escalated to upper management and was very frustrated. He threatened to kick the computer out on the street if we didn't send an expert to solve the problem.

At that time, magnetic media was in the shape of a disc and came packaged in a disc or disk cartridge of one to many platters. Rotating magnetic media at that time was 14 inches wide, and each was coated with a rust-colored material that had ferromagnetic particles suspended in a thin rigid layer on the surface. As a tiny electromagnet flew over the media on a microscopic layer of air as the media was spinning, it would "read" or "write" a pattern of 1s and 0s on a location. The location was called a sector and was addressed by a platter, cylinder number, and sector number which was a relative location from the index mark around the track. Each sector had parity written at the end of the pattern of 1s and 0s. Our disk drives had five disks with nine recording surfaces and one servo platter. It was called the Trident Disk drive and retailed for many tens of thousands of dollars in the 1970s. It could store between 25 and 100 MBs of formatted data. The servo platter could only write during formatting[11].

Late one night, we were working through midnight in the banking customer office building in Copenhagen, Denmark when a man in a tuxedo entered the room and just stood there with a look of concern on his face, not saying a word. The local service guy and I were busy inspecting all the hardware looking for a problem that caused the error and didn't speak to the tux guy for a while. We had the computer in pieces spread around the small room (an office converted into a computer room). We finally

---

11. Search for "history of hard disk drive" for more information.

asked him what he was doing. He said he was there to make a nightly system backup, and if he didn't, he could be fired. He said it was urgent because the security alarm would sound if we were not out of the building at a certain time. We quickly put the system back together so he could start the backup, which took several hours. I enabled the system log so I could capture more detailed data when it failed.

The next morning, I analyzed the log and found that the disc error had occurred because of a memory parity error when the disk controller read information from memory that needed to be written or backed up to the disk. Actually, the memory parity error had occurred during the backup which writes to the disc, but the customer didn't know it had failed during the backup. He only saw the error when trying to restore the backup. The backup utility was not checking for memory errors from the disc controller, only disc errors.

The memory error didn't occur at the same place each time it failed. However, there was one thing in common with all the error addresses: It happened on an address boundary between two 16KB RAM blocks.

I knew where to look inside the error log to obtain the failing address of the error.

When the customer wrote his program, he defined a block of memory space for temporary storage. There was an option when defining the block to initialize it with zeros, a user list of numbers, or nothing. He chose nothing[12]. Well, that normally would not be a problem because usually, a program would write something to RAM first before reading it. However, this customer used the buffer to write data in a length of 8-bit bytes. Our CPU memory interface could access the RAM in 8-bit bytes or 16-bit words. However, the disc controller memory interface could only access the RAM using a 16-bit access. The sectors were a length of 128

---

12. Most programs I was familiar with always chose the default of zeros.

bytes of user data each with parity written also at the end. If the disk controller got a RAM parity error while reading RAM and if it wrote to a disk sector, it would terminate the write immediately and not finish writing the sector with its parity.

When the customer program loaded, it was supposed to initialize the RAM with something to ensure all the bytes had good parity, except for the temporary buffer that had no default initial value. If the starting address of the loaded program was aligned just right, as the program wrote the last byte using the CPU as the bus master to the RAM, it only wrote the next-to-last byte on a 16 KB RAM block. The last byte was never written, which shouldn't cause a problem because it should already be initialized. When the disk controller tried to copy the RAM data to disk and was told to include the next-to-last byte, it had to include the last byte also because of the 16-bit access limitation. The disk controller got a parity error on the RAM access. When the disk controller got the parity error during the write to disk, it immediately aborted and left a fatal disk parity error on the incompletely written sector. The customer data was still there; I could manually read it from the disc. The data written was good; it just had bad parity. I could rewrite the sector and the restore could finish[13].

I called my friend Kirby Kyle, our lead software developer, at HQ, and we found a coding error in our own program that loaded the RAM initially. It was supposed to initialize the entire RAM but calculated the last address of each 16KB block incorrectly by one 16-bit word. The bug was created when the 16KB RAM modules were added to our product. The code used a loop instruction, which decremented a counter until it reached zero. The counter was set to the binary equivalent of 16KB divided by two because it initialized two bytes per write. If the counter was non-zero, then it wrote to the RAM address, which then incre-

---

13. Search for "history of disk data recovery" for more information.

the RAM address by two and decremented the counter by one. When the counter reached zero, it skipped to the next block until all blocks were written.

Unfortunately, the last 16-bit word of the 16KB block was skipped when the loop count reached zero. The person coding it put the check for zero before the RAM write instead of after. The problem would only be seen if a customer program did a byte-write to the next-to-last 16-bit location in memory. That was an easy fix.

Luckily, few customers had programmed like that. I never received word that they accepted the computer, and I never heard from them again. Sometimes it's not in your best interest to reveal your bugs to your customers. I did stay in touch with the local service guy[14].

Modern computers need to perform a memory clear before loading programs to prevent parity or ECC errors.

SETTING UP FOR SUCCESS

What can we learn from this?

Help desks need strict organization and a crack team to help them function correctly. The errors found in the software were unfortunate, but we were still able to find a solution by following clear organizational standards at my company. Here are some pointers to help you organize your own help desk.

Help Desk Managers

SEND SURVEYS TO YOUR CUSTOMERS ABOUT THEIR HELP desk experience and get feedback about the solution offered. Your

---

14. By the way, in Denmark, a "cup of coffee" is actually espresso: very, very strong coffee.

company can more easily find solutions if they know where a chink in the help desk chain is lacking.

Identify cases where the "fool-proof solution" didn't fix the problem. Product design problems are rare but will show up as unsolved customer issues. Identifying them and fixing them quickly is critical to company success.

Set up a system to better train help desk agents to understand problems. Sometimes, the call center database cannot match similar calls because the customer describes the same issue differently or the help desk pro categorizes the issue differently. In the absence of a team leader who encourages help desk people to communicate with each other about common problems, you are at the mercy of the database. No one would ever guess that a disk parity error was caused by a software problem.

Product Quality Professionals

NEVER ASSUME A SYSTEM TEST IS AS GOOD AS OLD-fashioned sub-testing, especially when new components or features are added. Sometimes, new code breaks something else.

Recognize that there are limitations in system testing. If you're too broad in your focus, you can miss entire applications. There are occasionally subtle bugs hidden in the code that can derail entire systems. When you do detect problems due to improper testing, fixing the issues is time-consuming, and you may need to travel to make customers happy. Remember that you're not just testing products to fulfill requirements on the organizational, national, or even international level. More work now means less work later.

Product Development Professionals

IMPLEMENT GOOD DESIGN REVIEWS AND SOFTWARE functional verification tests. Double-check your code and document the expected inputs and outputs to make it easier for someone else to find mistakes or to implement changes without errors. The more you document about your processes, the easier problems can be solved.

Modern logic verification tools can measure toggle rates and estimate coverage, but it's garbage-in garbage-out (GIGO). A logic signal can toggle, and still get the wrong answer. Create comprehensive test case designs to catch problems early. Practice scenario analysis by thinking like an end-user. Even consider crowdsourcing testing to uncover problems you hadn't originally considered. Modern tools allow you to automate test generations that explore potential customer inputs you hadn't considered and help you anticipate failures.

Remember that initial testing, even if it's extensive, shouldn't be the end of your testing methods. Develop metrics that will help you recognize when potential problems occur. And be creative! There are always solutions to problems, even if they're not easy.

Product Managers

ALWAYS HAVE A SYSTEM DEBUG GUY ON STAFF TO analyze system failures and provide feedback to design teams to fix and implement procedures to prevent similar problems in the future. A debug guy can move in between teams to better understand how products work. They can open the lines of communication between the development team and the customers so permanent solutions can be found.

Establish clear documentation and knowledge-sharing procedures to make it easier to communicate between departments. Letting members of the development and product teams know when there are problems and when you're using your debug guy can give your company a better way to communicate. It'll also streamline your testing strategies to prevent further bugs.

Legal Team

ESTABLISH LINES TO HELP YOUR STAFF IN LEGAL pickles. Product safety issues may require a field recall. The help desk may not know a particular customer complaint indicates a serious safety issue. Your database should be capable of parsing the calls to look for potential safety issues.

As the legal team, you're responsible for streamlining customer success strategies in recalls, so set up a method to make recall scaling easier. Set up rapid response teams to perform legal and public relations backflips if necessary. If the issue is widespread, setting up the right organizational paths to follow helps your organization save face and produce a much better product.

CHAPTER NINE
GARBAGE IN, GARBAGE OUT

SID LEISNER WAS ONE OF THOSE GUYS THAT COULD completely derail any meeting. I cringed whenever he attended one of my status meetings, and he avoided attending when I specifically requested to drill down into what might be a bug in his design. Sid used the "f-word" in almost every sentence and spoke in a loud, intimidating voice with ultimate confidence, challenging anyone to confront him. He also had a reputation for verbally abusing people whom he considered intellectually inferior, or at least that was my impression. He deflected justified criticism by exaggerating praise upon his accuser, making it extremely difficult for anyone to get him to accept responsibility for his mistakes.

Sid was different around the higher management than he was around his coworkers. You might say he knew how to kiss the right butts. He also let things get under his skin, and if he was particularly mad at any one of his coworkers, he would let them know. It's why so many meetings were wasted[1].

---

1. To give him a bit of grace, I should mention that he was often under the gun for projects, and that can put even the nicest people on edge. When you feel like

Sid was the lead design engineer of Northbridge for our 7th generation x86 processors that used that Digital Equipment Corporation (DEC) Alpha control interface. It was so far behind schedule that Dave B.'s team, under the direction of Atish G., skunk-worked a field programmable gate array (FPGA) version of the Northbridge and motherboard for us to execute the silicon test plan for the new microprocessor. It ran slower than an application-specific integrated circuit (ASIC) but got the job done.

After the Northbridge design was finalized, and we sent test boards all over the world to industry press for technical review, we found out that the boards failed under stressful workloads.

A Ph.D. engineer from Russia who worked for me on the system debug team at the time, Alexander P., collected empirical data. He showed that the root cause of the problem was from simultaneous switching output (SSO) noise and could be avoided by adjusting the value of the termination resistor for the control bus signals.

I showed Alex's data to Sid and the board engineer Scott S. before the reviewer boards were shipped. They argued that the simulations showed no problem. This argument went on for months. I finally went over their heads to a vice president, and he supported Scott and Sid. I then walked into the senior vice president's office and showed Larry H. Alex's empirical data. He was fully aware of the failures observed with the new product. He looked me in the eye and asked if I believed this was truly the root cause and solution to the problem. I looked right back, took my badge off my shirt, put it on the table, and told him I'd bet my badge I was right. He picked up the phone and called the vice president, Rich H., and told him to do what Mike Choate said.

We sent an army of folks with soldering irons and resistors around the world to change the termination resistors on the

---

you need to deliver products in a short time frame, it can get stressful. Name was changed.

control bus on these reviewer boards and it worked. We had a successful review and product launch.

SIMULATION DISSONANCE

The moral of the story is that simulation cannot reproduce what happens in real silicon. Simulation is only as good as the inputs; it can't manufacture a realistic output with unrealistic inputs. If the input variables are garbage, then the simulation is garbage.

But it's something that happens in every organization and industry. The success of a company depends on how much you're willing to put into it, and if you spend your time looking for shortcuts, your products will suffer. What you produce will be garbage. Some of the problems that arise from not simulating failures can be small, but many of the "small" glitches lead to something much bigger.

For example, on January 15, 1990, the AT&T Network collapsed for nine hours. The root cause for the problem was a single line of incorrect coding. It was used to control telephone switching for long-distance calls. A switch received from a maintenance code triggered the bug, and the entire system crashed. It sent messages to neighboring switches which started a cascading effect that caused a failure in the entire network and forced the shutdown of approximately 60,000 American lines. The "small" glitch led to major changes in regulation about testing large systems.

People easily forget that the reason many of these failures happen is because companies try to produce products too fast. Getting *something* out is better than getting nothing out to most people who are trying to meet deadlines.

But there are ways to make troubleshooting easier.

Before you send something out as "good enough," collect the facts. There are computer models today that make it much easier to identify problems before they occur, which happen at much higher frequencies.

MODELING FOR SUCCESS

As computers have become more advanced, simulation tools have needed to advance as well. Analog simulations now incorporate high-frequency signal propagation, which includes transmission line effects like reflections, loss, and dispersion. Computers are moving at such high frequencies now that it's impossible to measure everything like we did when I first worked with computers. The only way to properly simulate problems is through models.

They're essential for understanding how signals travel through modern computer systems. Below are some examples of modern models to improve simulations.

Mathematical Models

MATHEMATICAL MODELS ARE THE BASIS FOR CREATING all other models. They represent the physical and behavioral properties of electrical circuits at high frequencies. Measuring significant inductance in conductors at high frequencies helps engineers anticipate signal delays and ringing. Developing a model for capacitive effects predicts phase shifts and signal distortion. Also, catching resistive characteristics within mathematical models shows the correct paths to take when choosing the right substrates in a system.

Just like any other model, mathematical models require frequent updates. New components, designs, and regulations constantly evolve. Constantly extend your model to include any new complex behaviors or interactions.

Transmission Line Models

HIGH-FREQUENCY SIGNAL SIMULATIONS REQUIRE accurate modeling of transmission lines to describe how each signal moves through circuits. These models are the go-to simulations for modeling complex problems like reflections, loss, and dispersion.

Reflections happen when part of a signal reflects toward the source[2]. When the signal reflects, the signal slowly degrades until it's difficult for machinery to reach the original code. Modern transmission models can accurately predict these reflections based on the physical layout and properties of circuits.

High-frequency signals are susceptible to loss due to resistive and dielectric losses and the degradation of frequencies of different speeds can also be accounted for in transmission in modeling. How far a signal can transfer and the transitions between bits can be predicted by modeling dispersion effects on high-speed signals.

Trial and Error

SOMETIMES THE ANSWER IS OLD-FASHIONED TRIAL AND error. This can include modifying resistance, capacitance, impedance, or signal timing while testing signal response metrics. Systems face fluctuations in supply and demand often, so use dynamic adjustments in current or voltage in real-time. If you're still having problems, use a reference voltage[3] to manually see if there are fluctuations.

---

2. Reflections happen when there's an impedance mismatch. In other words, there's a connector or a change in trace width that is unaccounted for.
3. A reference voltage is a stable voltage level that can be used as a benchmark for adjustments. If the reference voltage needs to be extremely accurate so you can see any shifts in the voltage level of your simulation.

116 CHAPTER NINE

Of course, there are times when computers work (cease reporting errors) seemingly on their own, and that's not magic. Some variables changed and the problem will likely return.

PART TWO
A GUIDE TO INNOVATIVE DESIGN

CHAPTER TEN

INNOVATIVE TRAINING ELEMENTS FOR SOLUTION ENGINEERING TEAMS

My centralized debug team worked great as long as we focused on one program at a time from start to finish. Even though my team was highly skilled at multitasking by debugging several different issues simultaneously, as the company overlapped product development cycles with multiple projects without adding more resources, my team was viewed as a bottleneck, and it is almost impossible to predict a breakthrough on a tough issue that took days, and sometimes weeks, to reproduce a fail with debug instrumentation enabled. There were two major disadvantages to my centralized organization responsible for analyzing failures for multiple programs simultaneously during product development:

1. The design team/engineer that created the bug. They never felt any pain and, therefore, never learned from their mistakes and continued creating bugs. My team was doing all the dirty work for them. Often the engineer that created the bug had changed positions anyway by the time our feedback reached the design team.

2. Priorities clashed. Each program had its own product schedule and priorities for my team's assignments. Sometimes I was triple booked for meetings, so I had to delegate talented engineer resources to attend meetings for the team, which took them out of the lab. This made things worse by increasing the workload and pressure on the remaining engineers in the lab. If I had a backlog of ten unresolved issues, I preferred to work on the low-hanging fruit first: the problems we could resolve most quickly. However, the program wanted me to prioritize certain issues they needed. It was difficult to argue with that, but it caused my backlog to grow and made us look bad.

The company also shifted a lot of the testing and development work overseas, and I was pressured to develop a debug team there. I could do that if I could grow the team organically from the start of the program, but they wanted us to take existing staff and train them as debuggers.

I found it difficult to teach critical thinking. We showed them steps one, two, and three for solving problems if we already knew the root cause. Still, if it was a new problem, they needed the fundamental design engineering knowledge to develop their own list of root cause theories and experiments to collect data to prove or disprove the theories[1].

I have been asked by engineering students how they could improve their critical thinking skills. I originally said that critical thinkers have inherent traits, but I have since come to realize that it boils down to a deep curiosity. Solving very complex puzzles as a hobby and focusing on learning how the correct answer works will improve your critical thinking skills.

---

1. We just couldn't do that starting in the middle of a program. Each issue is different.

INNOVATIVE TRAINING

Innovation in engineering teams comes from training creativity. Because some people are naturally curious, it can be easy to teach them how to focus their curiosity on fixing problems or creating experiments to determine root causes. It all comes down to how much you're willing to invest in your team.

Deep-Dive Lectures

The problem with only listening to the people who work with you is that ideas and different thinking styles can become stale. If you've heard Dan give the same solutions to problems that he has for the last five years, you'll get stuck in a rut. The solution is to borrow the ideas of others by attending lectures.

Webinars are making lectures a lost art. So many of them are done online, and you just don't get the same level of understanding when you're not attending them in person. Showing up in person to lectures gives you and your team a chance to open a forum on the intricacies of a system you and your team are working on. Brainstorming after a complex lecture lets the information sink in as you learn to adapt to changes over time.

New Features

COMPANIES ARE ALWAYS UPDATING COMPUTERS TO ADD new features, and deep dives into upgrades and new features of products can give your team a better understanding of how industry standards are changing. New features usually bring with them different approaches to problems and different contexts to problems.

Expressing how developer—in your company and outside it —rationalize their creations gives your team a better understanding of how to improve system designs. Designers of new features can also show their practical applications, which are invaluable in helping the team find ways to use those upgrades. Live lectures give your team a chance to air out their thoughts and suggest improvements in an innovatively charged atmosphere. It's much easier to innovate when everyone in the room feels the excitement.

Bug Discovery, Design Changes, and Known Issues

UPDATES ON DESIGN CHANGES, BUG FIXES, AND THE methods used to discover hidden issues keep the conversation going across teams. Block architects and support leaders in development teams should understand what system design changes are made inside and outside their team's scope. Create a clear list or searchable database of resolved problems and unresolved test issues that are still in the system and encourage anyone to make notes on the running list of bug fixes to facilitate effective product support during manufacturing testing.

Be realistic when offering suggestions on how different teams can implement your bug fixes. Realize that not everyone knows what's going on in your lab, and the way you approach a problem is different than anyone else. Be patient in open lectures and create an environment of transparency that encourages anyone to ask questions.

Capabilities and Limitations

GET LECTURERS IN YOUR COMPANY AND EXPERTS FROM the companies that provide the basics for your systems to give answers to basic questions. They can give your team a better understanding of the software and let you know what the system can and can't do. They can also give insight into how you can use the system better.

Encourage lecturers to explain the tests that have already been given to the system, so you and your team know any chinks in the system's armor. It shows your team the scope of the system so you can be more realistic about your approaches. This is a great point to ask questions about simulations done on the system. If the system failed tests or if simulations weren't given, you and your team can give them instead.

Error Detection, Reporting, and Handling

THERE ARE ALWAYS NEW ERROR DETECTION techniques and software available on the market. Guest lecturers visiting your company and speaking during conventions can help you and your team get real-time answers for innovations in detection.

Error detection requires quick and efficient reporting. Many companies don't have the communication systems set in place to quickly share information about error detection and handling. If your team doesn't know the problems they could encounter when they work on a system, they can't be as effective in making changes. Your company should have rules in place to make reporting easy. Enforcing the rules by having lecturers visit you and your team periodically can help your team operate more effectively.

Use those same methods when handling the errors. When you are only exposed to the same people and the way they solve errors, it's hard to be innovative when coming up with new techniques. Lecturers from different backgrounds can share their own techniques for handling errors and encourage your team to look at problems differently. Sometimes all it takes is a new pair of eyes on the problem to find a solution. You won't know what you're missing if you don't talk with someone outside your current team.

Debug Widgets and Feature Control Bits

LECTURERS WHO FOCUS ON THE MORE NUANCED controls over systems through debug widgets and feature control bits can give insights into how to make debugging even more hands-off. They can also show how new software improves troubleshooting and performance. Again, listening to someone with an outside perspective can encourage your team to come up with their own solutions.

Test Coverage

THE NEW FEATURES IN SYSTEMS MAKE IT NEARLY impossible for tests to cover everything before it's released. It's why there are so many bug fixes after product releases today. Symposiums that are designed to teach designers and engineers what was covered and what wasn't in simulations help teams become more prepared when debugging. These lectures should include in which scenarios systems were tested, the outcomes of those tests, and the limitations highlighted. Look for people who emphasize the good and the bad of system designs.

These lectures also give your company more insights into a system's reliability. If some companies aren't doing enough testing before they send their systems, you can predict the potential problems and missed simulations to adjust in your company. Some companies aren't upfront about the limitations of their systems, so participating in lectures with more transparent people can make innovation in your lab much easier.

. . .

Bug Database Review

One of the biggest sources of information we have today is archived data. But, we usually have so much data, and many companies let it sit in a file and no one analyzes it. Plus, if you don't know what you're looking for, the amount of data can be very daunting! But, instructing your team on how to use the data and focusing on some metrics over others can give your team invaluable training to deal with any new problems that arise within new systems.

Historical Bug Analysis

YOUR TEAM PROBABLY ALREADY LEARNED HOW TO detect bugs if they're new hires, and they've likely seen many of their own if they've been on your team for a long time. To make your team even more effective, use historical bug analysis to reveal more patterns than what your team has experienced. Find out which type of testing showed the bug by looking through automated testing, manual quality assurance (QA), user feedback, and simulation results.

When you find the bug, dig into the root causes. Are there coding errors, design flaws, team miscommunications, or a failure to follow requirements? What problems did these bugs cause and are they costing the company money? When a consistent root cause comes out, gather your team to talk about how you can avoid these problems in the future. Create a strategy as a team to assign problems to multiple people. Conduct team meetings that brainstorm how to find solutions to some of the most common problems.

Opening the forum up to other teams in your company can encourage leaders to create regulations to make sure the same bugs don't keep happening. Collaborate between teams to educate each other on how to best approach some of the most common problems.

Major Function Risk Assessments

EVERY SYSTEM HAS ITS OWN SET OF RISKS IN A SYSTEM'S operations. Routinely break down systems into major functions to find out which risks pose the greatest threat to your systems. There are always some functions that are more prone to risks than others which should already be revealed when you do your historical bug analysis.

Develop a system that predicts where debugging efforts are necessary using metric tools and experiences within your team[2]. If you know your system well enough, use the information you've already gathered to create a report of the problems. Also, use the information from common trends in your industry to come up with a list of standard failures and inform your team of changes that need to be made. In case of failure, you can use the information you've gathered to come up with quick solutions to your problems.

Document all the steps you took to debug a system. Future teams and engineers can use your records as training for other departments.

Create Subprojects

IT'S EASIER TO CATCH BUGS (AND EASIER TO TRAIN your team on how to avoid them) if each project is broken into

---

2. Make sure you know the capabilities of your tools. If you have an existing tool that can give you answers and solve problems, use it. If you need a different tool, make sure you've made enough room in your budget to either make it to get it.

parts. Create a list of all the bugs found in each subproject and use them to predict possible failure rates based on historical failure rates.

It's important to remember that logic simulators can't catch all the possible bugs, so the more you isolate, the faster they are to fix. Spend resources to help your team know what they're looking for when catching bugs. Include each subproject and its corresponding topic to show how each interacts with one another. Open the floor to engineers with unique ideas and ask how they debug software in each subproject. If they recognize the tell-tale signs, they can develop more creative solutions.

Toggle Coverage vs Sequence Coverage

Many companies are hyper-focused on toggle coverage in their training. When you measure toggle coverage successfully, you can ensure all your designs are functional by catching where some signals are static and untested. It's an effective and fast way to make sure you're covering all dormant bugs before you send your products out the door. But it's not the only metric that is essential in creating a long-lasting product.

Sequence coverage provides a deeper understanding of verification. It makes sure the design's behavior aligns with how it was intended to operate. If you focus more on how the product is designed, you'll catch more bugs that pop up when customers use it. You can see how products will be used by customers by providing different scenarios and seeing how they play out. You might even catch some rare event sequences that only pop up in real-world applications.

When training for sequence coverage, focus on scenarios that apply to real life. What bugs have you seen pop up in some of the most ordinary uses of your products? It makes your team stretch themselves. If you can see outside what happens in the lab, you're more likely to come up with creative techniques to solve problems. You're also more adaptable when there are problems that don't initially pop up in simulations.

These methods can be more effective than artificial intelligence (AI) at catching problems that haven't already come up in simulations[3]. Although AI is extremely advanced, it's not infallible. It has limited knowledge of context-specific bugs because it doesn't have the information necessary to make accurate decisions—at least not yet. Because it's constantly improving, AI prediction will improve with it. But until that happens, it's best to combine AI with traditional approaches to catch the most bugs.

Cross-Team Training

Cross-training with design teams and product engineering teams involves swapping team members with different roles to learn how each department works. The new team members get to see how different departments handle failures and the steps they take to fix them. Over several weeks, team members will better understand the company they work at and can be more effective when they return to their original teams.

As far as I'm aware, cross-team training is very underutilized. It's been invaluable in helping my team learn more, and it's the perfect way to stir up new ideas and encourage better communication between departments. It's one of the easiest ways to help your team learn, but so many companies don't use it. I've seen teams vastly improve their productivity because of their experiences in other labs. They can act on new skills and provide insights they might not have considered if they'd stayed where they were. Your company will see technical advancement through the people who experience things in all parts of your company.

---

3. AI analyzes data already available, so it doesn't include new bugs that haven't been seen before.

Recognizing Effort

AS MUCH AS WE'D LIKE TO SEE THE HEROES OF EACH team get the recognition they deserve, the truth is that sometimes they're overlooked, especially if they're frontline employees or people who work in the background. The recognition that team leaders can give only goes so far, and most of the time upper management doesn't always see the efforts made.

Worse yet, these very valuable team members can become crutches for their teams; team leaders may always depend on them for innovative designs. Upper management usually only wants to hear the good news, so if an employee is always pulling more than his or her own weight, they might not be recognized[4].

Giving team members the chance to work in other departments can allow them to shine and get better recognition for their work. When they're gone from their departments, most of the time they're seen for how valuable they are. It's a great exercise to help leaders realize that they're not doing their best to recognize the people who do the most work. It might sound brutal, but sometimes if practices are so bad that they're not recognizing the best people on the job, it might be time to amputate by sending your employees to other departments so upper management can get a better idea of who they have on their teams.

Once you discover the chinks in your methods for finding the most valuable people on your team, make a conscious effort to include recognition in your training. Create a strategy to help both team members and management feel comfortable recog-

---

4. Of course, that really depends on the manager. Some managers are very good at recognizing talent, but if they're not getting all the information about those who work under them, it's easy for them to overlook things.

people who have gone above and beyond. The more you recognize your team, the more they'll do for you.

Cross-Departmentally Bartering

SOMETIMES WHEN DEPARTMENTS HAVE CREATED THEIR "dream teams," they'll be very hesitant to make trades for other teammates. New people coming into their teams don't always have the same training and often have different ways of doing things. Though there's a theoretical improvement that comes with cross-departmental training, it's hard to convince other team leaders to get on board.

So, instead of demanding a change, give them something in return. Give team leaders the chance to pick where they want their team members to go to get the best training. Let them know that they can expose their employees to things that will benefit their team overall.

Not enough companies emphasize how important it is to let their teams experience new things. If you're relying on one team member to do the majority of the heavy lifting, it's easy to forget that they need to grow, too. The more chances they get to try new things and work through problems differently than the methods in your department, the more useful they'll be to you and your team, which is an excellent selling point for cross-departmental training.

CHAPTER ELEVEN
INNOVATIVE TOOLS FOR POST-SILICON SOLUTION ENGINEERING

POST-SILICON SOLUTION ENGINEERING IS ESSENTIAL IN making a finished product work effectively. Over the years, I've seen many companies fail to implement the right tools or focus too much on the wrong ways to handle solution engineering. Here are some suggestions to make post-silicon solution engineering much more effective.

DEBUGGING TOOLS OVERVIEW

Debugging is essential to all processes in post-silicon production, and if you're a student or an engineer, you've probably already seen some of these before. If you're creating your own systems, it's important to keep each of these in mind. In the end, you'll create a much more reliable system.

PROTOCOL ANALYSIS TOOLS

Protocol analysis tools are responsible for the analysis and optimization of communications in control buses. They're essential in complex systems involving data transmission, signaling protocols, and system interactions to make semiconductor devices more reliable.

Internal control buses exchange data and signals between a variety of components within a system and are responsible for protocol analysis. They make sure that information is transmitted correctly and monitor data integrity, signal timing, and error detection. If you set up internal control buses properly, they can detect problems before they get worse. If you're constantly running into optimization problems, you can use internal control buses to fine-tune data transfers to improve the performance of your systems. Some of the most common industry standard buses are memory interfaces, PCI interfaces, USB, and network interfaces, all of which are customized to be as complicated as the product that you're trying to sell. They serve as the basis for more complicated semiconductor systems, but they require a lot of analysis to make sure they work.

It's hard to predict how much you need to invest in both your company and outsourcing resources to pay for external protocol analysis tools for control buses. Investing is a long-term solution, so it's hard to know if you've budgeted enough. It always seems like there's never enough money in a budget to account for just how many internal control buses you'll need, which is why most companies underestimate how much to allocate to protocol analysis tools.

Developing a Long-Term Strategy

SHORT-TERM SOLUTIONS WON'T COVER PROBLEMS WITH a long-term strategy, so make room to put proactive resources in place. Regularly check the performance of your analysis tools and have teams document when there are flaws or when the system seems to be slowing down. Your main goal is to make sure the system is reliable and stable over a long period of time, so if you notice bottlenecks, report them to upper management as soon as possible.

Plan on scaling what you need years before you need it: If you plan on growing the size of your system in a few years, put more money in the budget to pay for internal protocol analysis tools. The truth is that not setting that money aside could slow up operations for years. Slowed analysis also means that you can't check for performance, and your competitors could offer better products while you're trying to figure out the small problems first. If you have the right strategy in place, you can prevent issues before they ever come up or fix unknown problems before your customers realize it.

Collaborating Development

EVEN AFTER YOU INTERNALLY MAKE SURE YOUR analysis tools are up to speed, you can still run into problems. The resources you need to make internal control buses can weigh you down, and if you spend too much on them, you won't have anything left in your budget for other developments. So, sometimes the best option is to look to external sources to collaborate on tool development.

Look for external partners that have domain-specific information and experience that you don't have access to. Allow the engineers in other companies to use some of your internal control bus technology as well. Most of the time, collaboration means you have more access to different approaches and fresh perspectives. Working together means that you can combine resources to create tools even better than what either of you had.

Collaboration sometimes means you can get more comprehensive features for your internal control buses. The functionalities and features you didn't have the resources for could be essential to an external provider, so always do your research.

Usually, your company has something to offer other companies, so create a barter-like system to keep both sides happy.

Use your collaboration as the starting point for quality assurance. Once you've created something you're happy with, send it to an external team to get feedback and use that feedback to make quick changes. Outsource some of the processes your company doesn't have time for to external partners who specialize in those testing techniques. It can save your company time and money to set up collaborations with the right companies.

High-Speed Oscilloscopes

Much like protocol analysis tools, high-speed oscilloscopes are essential for analysis, debugging, and optimizing the performance of semiconductor systems. They offer a look into signal behavior and can diagnose difficult (if not impossible) issues by using a manual analysis tool. If you can use them in your design, they're well worth the investment.

One of the best uses for high-speed oscilloscopes is for debugging. They catch problems that come from small issues like noise or tiny vibrations. They're much better at finding solutions to problems quickly, and if your system is already prone to issues from small vibrations, you can catch bugs before they're sent out with the product.

But, like protocol analysis tools, they are also expensive and hard to fit into budgets. You need to plan to include them in your systems long before they are necessary. They're popular among companies who are very invested in making sure their products are of the highest quality before they leave the factory, but that can mean that high-speed oscilloscopes are hard to come by. It's definitely worth it to add them to your budget, but it can be hard to convince decision-makers to pull the trigger, especially if they're just looking at their bottom line.

But there are ways to make sure that you can add high-speed

oscilloscopes to your list of tools. It just takes smart planning to make sure you can stretch the resources.

Thinking Long Term

Start with encouraging your team to make a reserve fund. If you already have an idea how many you'll need to diagnose your system, set a budgetary minimum and create a reserve of more cash in case you need it. Adding a little extra money to the pot will give you a little wiggle room if there is a price increase or if there are other things you didn't see coming. The faster you can get these tools, the faster you can solve problems.

Look into research grants and private financing if you want to give your budget a boost when you're struggling with money. Just find someone on your team or in your company who knows how to write the perfect grants.

You can also use good old-fashioned know-how to find deals on acquiring high-speed oscilloscopes. Some companies offer discounts if you buy them in bulk, and you can always pool your resources with a partnering company if you're really struggling to get the funds.

Overcoming Limited Availability

If you've worked in the industry for a while or are an engineering student, you might already know that high-speed oscilloscopes can be hard to come by. They're very specialized, and because the cost to manufacture them is high, they come with a high price tag. They're also very valuable in all types of diagnosis, so a lot of companies want them.

If you can't find one on the market, one of your best bets is to find a partnering company that is willing to lease you their tools for a discounted price. Sometimes it makes sense to develop your relationship with other teams and companies if you can find a deal that will make it beneficial for both of you—working side by side with another company that can complement your work and speed up the efficiency of your systems.

Diagnostics Software

Diagnostics tools are at the heart of creating useful post-silicon tools that take your products to the next level. Testing products before they're put into production can save you a huge headache. Post-silicon solution engineering needs diagnostic tools to make sure projects stay on track, but some problems make integrating them into systems hard. For example, if you don't have the rights to license more effective software, it can get really expensive to use them in your products. If you're keeping to a budget, licensing can be more expensive than it's worth, which is why some companies only get by with the bare minimum.

When it comes to troubleshooting calls, there's always a big problem when customers call in with little to no idea what their problems really are. You might already have a script that takes you through what you need to ask to diagnose the problem over the phone, but if you can't see it for yourself, it's frustrating. Some of the time, you'll even go through the entire list of solutions and still have no idea what the problem is! Worse yet, if someone complains of a failure but can't make it happen again when you're on the phone, what do you do then? Many customers don't know the right questions to ask or even remember exactly how the failure occurred.

So, what's the solution? You need to be careful in how you approach adding diagnostics software to your products to make sure they follow regulations, but here are some examples of ways to incorporate diagnostic tools into your systems.

Getting Software Packages

SOMETIMES THE SIMPLEST SOLUTION IS GETTING AS much diagnostics software in a package as possible. You'll probably run into problems at some point if you're hunting for individual software you don't have. If you have the option, try to get packages.

If you're on the other end—creating software—consider selling your software in a set. You can license all the products under the same license, which can save your customers a lot of money. The more helpful you are to the people buying your software, the more likely you are to sell your products. Sometimes people see it as a price cut for their companies to give as much in your packages as possible, but you'll get many more return customers.

Seeing Your Customer's Problems

ANOTHER BIG PROBLEM WITH DIAGNOSTICS TOOLS comes when you're trying to find a solution to a problem that the customer doesn't know how to describe. And sometimes, when they try to recreate it, they can't make the problem happen again. You see this all the time in help desk centers that are trying to walk customers through how to fix problems just by listening to what the customer is telling them. The more information you have, the faster and more accurate you can be with your solution.

So, instead of relying on the customer, create a built-in diagnosis tool for the final product that is always reporting problems. If a failure happens, you can see the data you need from the first time it fails. You can investigate your customer's software's history and see the alerts that pop up when there's a problem.

Keeping an Open System

TOO MANY PEOPLE TODAY TRY TO HIDE WHAT THEY'VE made in background features. These hidden features can seem like they're saving your company a buck, but the problem comes when people are trying to diagnose your software. If there are hidden features that are causing a problem and help desk professionals don't know about them, they can't get their jobs done.

As a solution, keep all information out in the open and make it easy for anyone who buys your software to access it. Provide as much information as you can about all aspects of the design to people who need to know about it. Include notes in your software about possible problems and what you did to solve them. Most customers won't know the difference if they're given all the information, but it'll really help out the engineers who are working to find solutions to problems they don't know how to find.

PRE-SILICON DEBUGGING STRATEGIES

Of course, none of this is possible if you don't consider how these chips are made. These pre-silicon debugging strategies are the first steps in helping you mitigate problems that come up during simulations instead of when they're out in production. These strategies are important in making your computer robust by increasing the efficiency and accuracy of debugging processes you conduct after you've made your products.

Pre-Silicon Emulation Features

Pre-silicon emulation is the practice round for engineers that helps them test simulated versions of computer chips before spending a lot of money on fixing the problem. In essence, it gives you an insight into the chip's behavior before you send it out to market.

You can redesign problems as part of your pre-silicon emulation system to include input from both software and hardware teams. The pre-silicon emulation stage means you need to collaborate with other teams to see how well the software and hardware will mix.

But there are design elements you need to consider when you add these new features. The complexity of the emulation model can change how effective your performance is, so create an emulation model that fits the chip's design. Make sure your system can validate and verify problems consistently; a debugging strategy that doesn't tell you exactly where the problems are is useless. Lastly, make sure your tests will fit in with your system before you start to create them and check with all teams that work on the system before you get started.

Custom "Debuggable" Motherboards

These motherboards are equipped with comprehensive test points that help engineers see into a chip's behavior and use diagnostics during the early stages of development. They're designed by putting an array of test points at key locations on the motherboards, which makes it easier for engineers to access. Engineers can then see the most important signals, interfaces, and components of each system. If they're placed correctly, they can make identification and isolation of issues very easy to detect early.

Think about custom "debuggable" motherboards as the perfect place for monitoring a system's behavior without stopping any processes that are currently running. It's the perfect plug-in place for tools like oscilloscopes and diagnostic instruments to take a snapshot of the signals as they flow through the motherboard. If you can, pinpoint problems immediately to make troubleshooting much easier for engineers.

With the right collaboration between teams, "debuggable" motherboards give you the chance to share insights with other teams. It's the perfect opportunity to swap people in your team to give them experiences working on the same project but with different team members. Most of the time, creating a plan for systematic testing is complex, so switching things up is more beneficial to you. It allows you to ask questions and add more perspectives. If you can, you should ask people from outside the traditional post-silicon engineers to join your team, which can give you insight into how to continuously improve your design process.

The biggest problem with creating custom "debuggable" motherboards is knowing where to put the mid-bus probes. You have to get the right types of connectors and routing to make chips work properly, so it takes a lot of design time. But, to solve that problem, consider making the interfaces very visible, and add as many as possible, within limits. Solving the problem this way supports both the debug and solution engineering teams. There are tradeoffs depending on what you're creating, so you'll have to make a judgment call on what is possible.

Custom System BIOS with Debug Capability

Like the other two methods in this section, custom system basic input/output systems (BIOS) are one of the best ways to analyze and troubleshoot problems. They help you refine functionality within the system before you actually start to make products. You can monitor system initialization processes and ensure that hardware configurations and firmware interactions are doing what they're supposed to in real time. It's a real-life scenario test that can give you a better idea of what your customers will do and the problems they'll create.

Custom system BIOS with debug capabilities allows you to record system activities, how they're performed, any sequences, and hardware problems that occur when starting up. It's essentially the starting point for engineers to find out how code flows through the system and helps them identify bottlenecks and their root causes. It's a great tool to combine with other debugging strategies. Think of this capability as a basic system to boost the motherboard. It provides signals to indicate which components to replace.

The problem is that many sellable products often hide new features that aren't controlled by the operating system. It gives people the opportunity to customize their offerings to match their performance marketing, but these capabilities are often turned off for power saving or customization. It's done to make sure that end users don't mess up the machines, but you have to reconfigure them so they're accessible to professionals.

The solution is to add software features that allow debuggability or control knobs to turn on and off for professionals. Android has systems like this that allow you to turn advanced features off and on. Most people don't even know about the advanced features, so it's a great way to have an accessible system without letting an end user mess things up. Unfortunately, for most companies, it's a major investment, and a lot of them won't add debuggability to override certain settings for customization.

POST-SILICON DEBUGGING TECHNIQUES

Once you've made it past the debugging strategies, it's time to implement them in real time. As you refine your designs, use several debugging techniques to ensure the integrity and functionality of the chips you've created. Even if you have a very extensive production testing system, the systems you have in place can't predict everything, which is why testing after production is so important. These techniques provide the perfect way to diagnose, analyze, and then rectify any potential problems you've found post-silicon.

JTAG Wigglers

Joint test action group (JTAG) wigglers are hardware tools to help debug post-silicon products and to test semiconductor devices. You can plug these devices into JTAG port interfaces on circuits that support them which allows you to access and manipulate the components of the chips when you diagnose them.

JTAG wigglers are a great tool for boundary scan testing how components are connected within a chip. They offer a lot of advanced features that can help you identify where there are problems in connections and find possible solutions quickly. You can stop processes, inspect the internal states, and modify registers to diagnose the problems that come up to optimize the chip's behavior.

You can create test patterns and monitor the signals to see if those paths are correct. From there, you can assess if the chips are functioning properly. If they're not, JTAG wigglers can narrow down exactly where the problem is in the hardware.

JTAG Control Software

JTAG control software also tests circuits, but, unlike the JTAG wigglers, they interface with semiconductor devices to improve the internal components of the chip. JTAG control software is much more focused on the user-centric approach that analyzes data that comes while testing the product while in use. It can also allow you to pause processes at set breakpoints, which lets you inspect the registers and analyze the trace data that comes from diagnosing complex issues.

The JTAG control software tests are very precise. They can perform targeted testing and troubleshoot the processes when problems come up. If the system shows multiple problems, using JTAG control software can break down the trends and verify the

INNOVATIVE TOOLS FOR POST-SILICON SOLUTION ...   143

responses. The more the software knows, the better it can automate analysis in the future.

JTAG control software is part of the heavy-duty quality checks. You need to make sure your systems are meeting operational requirements, and using the software is an easy way to make sure they're streamlined and precise.

Scan Dump Capture and Automated Analysis

Scan dump captures let you take a closer look into the internal states of products and register their values and signal responses when you're debugging. It provides a snapshot of the product's behavior and how it operates at specific points in time. It's key for randomly observing what's happening in the system, but it's also helpful when you know exactly when failures are occurring. Most systems don't have a way for you to start and stop the clock, which is why scan dump captures are so important. If there are issues or anomalies during regular operations, scan dump captures can track those changes and help engineers make changes before the product is sent out.

Scan dump simple designs can run simulations up to a point and tell it to stop the clock and send another signal to shift the current state of the transistors into a separate register called the scan flop. From there, you can shift them out in a serial chain to analyze the internal state of change of the product. It's the perfect way to help you see how the design works over time and compare the results to optimize the design. Advanced machines can stop the clock, but the problem is that, if you stop on a failure, it'll change your results significantly. But, stopping the clock as close to failure as possible can give you a lot of information. If possible, capture information at various checkpoints without stopping the clock and compare it to the expected behavior of your products.

When scan dump data comes through, automated analysis can scan what's given based on algorithms the engineering team puts together to recognize patterns and common anomalies. The automated processes make it easier to flag problems based on criteria that you already defined and prioritize debugging techniques that are based on those insights. The more time you spend defining the right criteria, the faster you can make debugging decisions.

Once you've analyzed the data, suggest corrective actions to increase the performance of the system. Think about it as a final way to make sure your customers don't have to call the help desk when they have problems. The faster the product works, the fewer angry calls you'll get from people. To most people, fast computers mean more reliable products and higher quality, so it's worth the time to make sure the product is as optimized as possible.

DATABASE DESIGN FOR LOGGING AND TRACKING ISSUES

A well-designed database should include issue logging and tracking to make sure that bug information is organized so it's easy for engineers to see potential problems. The best database designs are easy to navigate and have plenty of notes specifically related to relational databases or NoSQL solutions. Add points of correlation to make it easier to see where there are multiple and continuous problems and make notes about how you fixed the problems.

Once you have a clear database design, identify and classify your information by related problems, severity levels, and prioritization. You can usually create tags to help you cross-reference the problems that have already come up in the system and track where they are in the process of resolving them. Keep everything in chronological order so you can easily see where things are in the process. Include the names or initials of the people or team working on each problem so it's easier to reach out to them to ask questions. If you're thorough enough, you can save time and money on quality assurance by just being quicker at resolving these problems. The extra work may seem like a waste of time, but once your production reaches a high enough level, it's well worth the effort.

DATABASE REPORTS

Create reporting and analytics to give your team a general look into the most common problems every week. This should be a part of your normal weekly training, so everyone is caught up on what other teams are doing. Open the floor up to everyone on any team that is involved in production. The open brainstorming session can give you more ideas than just keeping a running tab of all the issues.

Assign each team to create a report of their issue resolution metrics, which includes the number of issues, the time it took to resolve those problems, and any patterns that show where the problem has happened again. Tell each team to focus on bottlenecks and encourage everyone on the team to speak up when they think of more effective ways of dealing with common problems. Of course, that includes letting management know when they need more resources.

With a strict enough reporting structure, you can follow the problems back to design flaws or systematic failures and prevent them from reoccurring. Make a note of trends in your reporting and tell management and other teams when you think there are any potential issues when end-users start to use your products. If you see a problem that only occasionally pops up, add it to the notes of the software so future engineers can make changes. Let multiple teams look at the reports and make suggestions. The creativity of your team will improve decision-making in the future.

Use these reports to analyze your test coverage and root cause analyses. If you miss a test at any stage of the process, you can catch it before you send your products out into the market.

You can also catch if any underlying problems are causing the issues.

ADVANCED DEBUGGING FEATURES

Finding and fixing problems once they're in production can be tricky, which is why engineers usually implement advanced debugging features to make sure they're catching what's causing the issues. The faster you can find problems, the more efficiently you can change chip behaviors when more are put into production. These advanced debugging features are among the last features most companies use to make sure their chips are running perfectly.

Advanced Breakpoints, Triggering, and Tracing Capability

Trying to solve mysteries in complex systems is like trying to find a needle in a haystack. For example, think about a chip controlling an autonomous car. If the car stops responding, engineers need to break down what is causing the problems in the operation and find out where it's creating an unusual signal that's stopping the car's sensors. They can use the triggering mechanisms to collect data right before the problem happens and break down the decisions step-by-step. It's a long process if you're doing it manually, but using advanced systems can help you find solutions by process of elimination in a fraction of the time.

Integrating advanced breakpoints, triggering, and tracing capabilities directly into the hardware makes it easier to analyze the system's behavior and find problems. You can put breakpoints directly onto chips, which can pause the system under specific conditions so you can inspect the state of the system at precise times. You can also activate data collections for data capture without overloading storage resources. It makes internal operations more visible through tracing capabilities, and you can get a better idea of what's going on inside the chip.

You should also make the system flexible enough to see multiple logic functions simultaneously. The more flexible you are in diagnosing different issues across various parts of the system, the more secure you can make your systems. The increased flexibility creates secure access points for debugging security features, and these security measures often create more openings for engineers to access features without compromising the safety of the system.

The safety of the system often involves what happens during production. Picking the right advanced techniques can help you identify manufacturing issues. Occasionally, problems like misaligned components or soldering faults at critical points can cause a lot of issues. Setting breakpoints at well-functioning locations can help you isolate the anomalies and show you exactly where the manufacturing problems are. You can use the trace data to show irregularities in signal integrity and create specific steps that make it easier for engineers to fix in the future.

Advanced breakpoints can stop the system when timing problems are detected. You can use these stopping points to analyze why stops happen. It's also possible to create triggering points that can start recording when a problem occurs.

As more features are implemented, these complex systems often have problems with interconnected logic blocks, which can cause failures. When these blocks happen, you can set up advanced breakpoints that will capture the state of logic blocks when they fail. You can then use the data to reduce the noise and make sure all the interactions between logic blocks are working correctly. It's easier to see how complex interactions work within systems when the data can help you pinpoint trends and patterns over time.

. . .

Custom Debug IC Packages

Once you get your first silicon, you're going to find a lot of bugs. You can try debugging in simulations, but they're slow, and they don't show the big picture of what's happening in the entire system. Custom debug IC packages are more practical because you can embed diagnostic capabilities into the hardware, which gives you real-time observation and analysis.

You can access internal signals that show what's happening inside the chip when the bug happens by tapping into custom debug IC packages. They can monitor data flows, control signals, and clock cycles, along with other parameters that you set up. Because it's so customizable, you can choose which conditions you want to focus on to find the root cause and start debugging.

When you're designing your own system, you need to know the chip's behavior. Custom debug ICs can monitor clock signals to make sure that they're stable over time. Any changes in the clock can lead to timing problems that interrupt the typical operation of the system. The frequency of clocks has to be within a certain range to make sure they're operating effectively, and a closer look into the frequency helps you make sure it's aligned correctly.

These advanced systems also help you understand your hardware's operational flow. You can trace the paths taken by data as they move through various stages, letting you monitor it in real-time. If there are any disruptions in the flow, customized ICs can correct the commands. It makes the performance of your silicon much more reliable over time.

Finally, custom IC debug software helps you detect error signals by giving you immediate feedback. Problems like parity errors, checksum failures, or unexpected state transitions are immediately sent to you. You can create corrective measures that fix the problems that show up the most, stop redundancies, and mitigate the impact of errors.

Of course, there's a tradeoff for using advanced hardware.

Custom debug IC packages are usually very expensive, and they take a lot of custom hardware to support the advanced diagnostic features. It can also make your system much more complex to develop. But the more hardware you have to identify problems in your systems before you send them out, the more it'll pay off in the long run.

CHAPTER TWELVE

STAFFING FOR SOLUTIONS ENGINEERING

In my nearly five decades working in computers, I've come to realize that the most important thing in computing and companies is staffing. I have seen so many companies succeed when they depend on the right people for their staff. I've also seen companies fail because they don't hire the right people, or they don't reward the right people for their work. But how do you know exactly what you're getting when you recruit the people that you're looking for? You should always have recruiting goals and someone who manually looks at the resumes, but there's more to it than that.

I've found that there's a tried and true method to make sure that you are hiring the right people when it comes to solutions engineering. The short answer is that hiring the right people comes down to finding those who are willing to put in the extra work for you. And a lot of times you can't find that information just by looking at a resume. To keep you from getting bogged down with finding the right people for your solutions engineering, I've compiled a list of helpful tips to make staffing easy.

CHAPTER TWELVE

RECRUITING

If you've ever owned your own company, you've probably seen the importance of hiring the right people at the right time. The right person can make all the difference when it comes to how a company is run. That's why it's important to have recruiting goals: to provide a road map to complete the right steps in a company's progress.

But recruiting is only the first part of the process. You want to find the people who will help your team grow, but you also want to encourage them to stay on as long as possible. It all comes down to how you reward the people who are actually working for you and how you create a road map to help are recruits make a difference in your company.

Recruiting Goals

If you're looking for high achievements, you're also looking for overachievers and people who are willing to make their marks before they enter your company. You want to make sure that you are hiring people who are qualified and can handle the work over the long haul.

Be realistic when creating your recruiting goals. When you set your objectives make sure that you define a specific target for the roles know exactly when you want to have your recruiting process completed and the types of skills necessary to complete your work. All of this should align with what your company sees as the most important part of its values.

Determining how well someone will fit into your company is hard, especially if you don't have goals that are already outlined to help you find the right person. In the end, your goals not only help your company but also your future hires to make the best impact they can on the company. Recruiting the right person is a big deal, so here are a few ways to make it easier for you to narrow down the right people when you start hiring.

Highlighting Achievements

YOU CAN'T KNOW EVERYTHING YOU REALLY NEED TO know about somebody just from how well they did in school. But it is a good starting place to help you know exactly where your candidate comes from and what they have done in the past. For example, someone who has won a lot of scholarships, achieved a lot of academic merit awards, or has received special recognitions like Student of the Year can give you an idea if your potential hire is willing to go above and beyond your expectations. Ask previous employers or people who have worked with your potential hire if they are willing to go above and beyond to make sure that they are learning as much as they can.

Make a note if your potential hire is very consistent in what they do. It can be something as small as consistently showing up to work on time, or as big as constantly providing the company with higher and greater accolades. This is usually a good sign that you can depend on them to deliver quality results.

Your goals should also reflect leadership. Any time your potential hire shows up to manage or motivate peers is a good sign. Even if they haven't had a lot of experience in a working role, you can see if they have a combination of strategic thinking, effective communication, and a proactive approach if prioritize those questions when hiring them. Also, look for candidates who are willing to take the initiative to solve complex problems and find effective solutions.

Encouraging Curiosity and Thinking Critically

Curiosity is one of those things that most resumes don't capture. But if you talk to someone for long enough, you can find how well they seek out new information and how excited they are to make sure they can solve everyday problems. Look for someone excited to learn new things. Determine how willing they are to go outside of their comfort zones by asking them if they're willing to travel to conventions to learn about new engineering techniques and to hear from different people.

Ask your recruits if they are willing to try to learn new things through research. Use a common but complex problem to gauge how well your recruits are willing to research the problem and find answers that are beyond their current understanding. What kind of challenges did he or she face, and how did he or she go about finding solutions to those problems? Beware of candidates using the words "we did 'xxx';" drill down into the work they personally did.

When you're conducting initial interviews, or if you are talking to current employees, spend 10 to 15 minutes talking to them about their chosen research areas to find out how excited they are about them. The best people for the job are the ones who will spend the next few minutes talking your ear off about theories. The people who are the biggest assets to your company are the people who are deeply passionate about it, and they have a gift for sucking in knowledge and applying it later when complex situations come up.

Make it your company's goal to talk about complex engineering problems, even those not necessarily associated with your department. Sometimes the best problem solvers aren't the ones who got straight As in school, but the ones who use their time to create innovations and to try new things.

Hiring for Personality

STAFFING FOR SOLUTIONS ENGINEERING

AT THE END OF THE DAY, YOU HAVE TO WORK WITH THE people who you hire for a long time. That means you have to work with the quirks and the problems that come with differences in personalities and ways of thinking. The people who are going to stick around are the people who show that you won't quit when things get hard. So, one of the first questions you should ask is "What happens if someone says you can't do something?"

The people I wanted to hire are the ones who are looking to prove people wrong when they know they are right. Those are the people that are going to stick around. You can often find this personality trait in young people who feel like they have something to prove but don't rely on fresh graduates alone to give you that personality trait. To find somebody with that personality trait with a little bit more experience, talk with previous managers to find somebody willing to speak up when they encounter problems. I had very good success hiring new graduates who had previous intern experience.

But, if you're not careful, an abrasive personality trait can get you into trouble. Choose someone who has negotiation skills without access. For example, someone who challenges your knowledge or your authority constantly or resorts to anger to resolve problems is not the kind of person who will work well with the team. Hire somebody willing to work with you and not ghost you on problems that come up.

One of the biggest red flags is someone who seems to have a chip on their shoulder. They're the kind of person who thinks some jobs are just below them and they will reject them even if they need the experience. You see these kinds of people in all sorts of business, and they usually don't stick around for a long.

Engaging Talent

ENGAGING TALENT IS AT THE END OF THIS SECTION, BUT that doesn't mean it's not equally if not more important than the rest of the qualifications necessary for a good employee. When you hire anyone, you need to look for someone who can fulfill the tasks without feeling too overwhelmed. That means they need experience with complex systems and specifically key bus protocols.

When creating your recruitment goals, find key questions that will let you know if your candidate is prepared to take on some of the more difficult duties. Find out if they can communicate their successes and their mistakes in a way that shows you that they can handle difficult tasks associated with your brand and your company. One question you could ask is can you provide an example of a time when you used post-silicon engineering techniques to solve an unusual problem? This gives you a good gauge of their communication skills and if they can think critically enough to come up with an answer on the fly.

Remember that sometimes the best talent out there doesn't come from sources you would necessarily expect. I have found some of my greatest employees by recommendations from others, by looking through resumes that most people would throw out, and by sitting down and talking to people to find out more about them personally. You'll never know who can surprise you if you don't spend the time to learn about people through conversation.

Employment Process

It doesn't matter if you love it or hate it, resumes are a big part of finding the right people for your work. There are a lot of tools out there to help you analyze resumes without ever looking at them, but most of the time, you miss something with that process. Sometimes the people with the best resumes have the worst work ethic, and sometimes the people with the least experience have some of the most innovative ideas. You're missing out if you don't give each of them equal weight.

I've always found that slowing down the process is the best way to make sure that you're getting quality people. It takes more time, but it's worth it in the end. So how do you break down resume analysis?

My employer had a separate budget for college interns. I would typically get two or three engineering student interns per year. One time, I hired an intern who seemed to say all the right things during the interview, had good grades, and was likable, but on the job, even though he was enthusiastic, he acted like the job was in a country club; he came to work late, left early, always made excuses, asked for a lot of extra time off, and just didn't get any work done. I gave him multiple chances and tried to be patient, but when he broke an expensive tool for the second time, my patience was depleted. Patience is a virtue that can be owned by no man or woman, but you can rent it for a little while. I told him to pack his stuff and get out because I had a business to run, not a country club.

YOU'RE FIRED!

Two years later, at an intern appreciation party, he approached me and thanked me for firing him. He said it was the best thing that ever happened to him because he realized what he was doing was lazy and he didn't apply himself. He said he changed his ways and was graduating and had learned a lot since the firing.

Screening Candidates

YOUR FIRST STEP IN SCREENING CANDIDATES IS TO narrow down their resumes that just don't work. During the beginning phase, make sure that each candidate meets the minimum qualifications like education, certifications, and minimum years on the job. Some of the greatest people who apply just won't fit, and it's important to eliminate them early.

Because it's so easy to post a resume nowadays, you might get flooded with job applicants, so if you don't have the time to take an in-depth look at your candidates, a brief overview is sometimes the best way to go. If you're feeling overwhelmed with the number of candidates that you've gotten from posting a job, get other team members to help find the right person.

One of the biggest concerns I've seen nowadays is the number of people applying for jobs. Companies looking for remote workers may get thousands of resumes. It's tempting to sift through thousands of resumes with AI, but you might miss out on some great candidates. And AI can't detect everything. You may value some unspoken qualities in your company that don't show up on traditional resumes.

A few times, I volunteered to join the company recruiting teams to college campuses for job fairs, especially at colleges that had a good reputation for their computer engineering curriculum. After a trip to Florida, I had two openings for graduate students. I interviewed two students who were also best friends and college roommates in Florida. One said he wouldn't take the job unless I also hired his roommate. I liked them both, so I hired them both. It all turned out well.

Initiating Interviews

DURING THE INTERVIEW PROCESS, BREAK DOWN WHICH candidates most closely align with what you're looking for. Ask questions that relate to both their personality and resume, including their skills, experience, and technical qualifications. Ask critical thinking questions that are specifically important in your team.

Don't quickly push someone aside who might be a great

candidate but just doesn't fit all the qualifications for your team. You can always recommend the right people for other teams in your company. If possible, hop on the initial call with someone from another team who might also be interested in that candidate.

Also, during the initial call, find out your candidate's motivations[1]. This is also a great opportunity to find out what your candidate knows about your company and the role. If someone is wishy-washy about whether they want to join your company, they might provide vague answers to your questions, which can be a red flag. It's a great time for both of you to clarify any doubts or questions that either of you have about each other.

Ranking Candidates

YOU'LL ALWAYS HAVE A CLASSIFICATION OF GOOD, better, and best. As much as you might like someone as a person, they might not fit into the organizational culture or have the right skills you're looking for. Align any candidate with the goals you've created for the job. Think of all candidates as salespeople: Do you want to buy what they're selling? If not, it's best to move on to the next person.

Just like when you're initiating interviews, it might be helpful to add a team leader from another team to the hiring process. They can give you an outside perspective, and if you don't rank someone as highly on your list, that doesn't mean that the other team leader isn't more interested. Slow down and discuss the candidates at length. Find your top contenders, and continue to

---

1. While all companies want to think that their employees are interested in employment because they have an innate desire to work for your company at all costs, the truth is that many people are primarily in it for the money. So, don't be jaded when somebody tells you the truth.

narrow them down with additional interviews or internal discussions.

Hiring the Best

THE FINAL STEP IS TO INVITE THE PEOPLE WHO FIT THE criteria best to work for you. Compile a list of all their qualifications into a portfolio that you've created during their interview process and Sort people into positions that they best fill. Ask your candidates what they need to be the most successful at their new positions and try to accommodate their needs.

Remember that you might not have the final say in your favorite candidate. When I was interviewing a candidate for a new position, I found one that I thought would be perfect for my team. He had all the skills I wanted: he had critical thinking skills, and he was sharp as a tack. But, when I asked him to join my team, he said that he felt he fit better with another team instead. It was unfortunate, but I was still grateful he was working for my company and a team I collaborated with.

STAFF EXPERIENCE

Once you find the perfect person for a position, you've reached a milestone. But that's not the end of the discussion. The sad truth is that a lot of employees are not happy with their employment, and employers are to blame. In the last few years, there has been more turnover than ever before. Employees are becoming more comfortable with leaving their jobs if they feel the jobs are not satisfying their personal requirements.

There are a lot of theories out there to explain why many employers can't retain their employees. While I might not be an expert, in all my nearly half a century of work, I've seen what works and what doesn't. Your staff is the lifeblood of your company, so it's time you started thinking like that.

Employee Retention

Once you've found the right candidate, spend all your resources making sure that he or she is happy with that position. You should have a blend of education, monetary compensation, and benefits that will keep your employees happy. Make your employees skilled enough so that they can leave but make them happy enough that they won't want to.

Keep in mind that when most people leave a job, they're not leaving the work, they're leaving the manager. I've worked in a lot of places where I felt I could easily stick around because of the people, even if the work is difficult and demanding. But the flip is also true: I've had great experiences working at places that challenge me and provide great benefits, but I couldn't stay because the manager was terrible.

If you're a manager, become that ally. If you're hiring for a new position, show your candidates that you stick up for your employees and continue doing that after they've been they've been hired. It may not be fun to take the brunt of the blame or harassment from upper management, but your employees will remember it. Strong leaders are those who work with their team, not make their team suffer for them.

Develop connections with people that last a lifetime. I'm happy to say that there are many people in my past that I still consider close friends. These people are both managers and employees. I've been lucky enough to sit down with most of them and learn about them personally. Those connections are what keep people coming back to work. Even if you're working in a remote setting, make the time to learn about people and form those deep bonds. You'll never regret the time you spend.

· · ·

Company Culture

The distinction between employer and employee is becoming scarily more obvious all the time. After the COVID-19 pandemic, employees had a lot more say in how a company was run. The great resignation was a period of a couple of years when employees left their jobs if they felt they weren't treated properly or if they weren't making enough money. They wanted to work in places that suited them. The long and short of it is that company culture really matters.

One of the ways to improve company culture is to focus on employee engagement. Do employees feel like they have a say in the work they're doing? Do employees feel like they can offer advice to leadership? If they don't, you'll get high turnover rates. Employees want to feel like they can make a difference in their companies. And some of the most brilliant minds with the most interesting suggestions start at the bottom. If employees feel like they're not being listened to, they'll go to a company that *is* willing to listen to their ideas. The more employee-centric you can make your company, the happier your employees will be and the more your company will succeed.

Focus on creating a sense of belonging in the workplace. If your employees feel like they have a best friend at work, they are more likely to show up, and they are less likely to leave their jobs. Create scenarios where different groups of people can interact with each other about professional and personal things. Make your break room a place of open discussion. The more you allow people to talk to each other and the closer they bond, the happier people will be.

Also, making your workplace unique can be a fun way to engage employees. Your company's foundation came through struggle, and it came through countless stories of innovation in tech. Use your unique personalities within and without the job to make it welcome to your employees. Keep in mind that just because the unique personality of your company may seem less flamboyant than others doesn't mean your company isn't a place your employees love to be.

Make it a common practice in your business to keep work within the right confines. I can't stress this enough. Because so many people are going remote and because people are always accessible through phone, e-mail, or other messaging systems, it's easy to depend on your employees all the time. Instead, show your employees that they have freedom outside of the workplace. Customers are demanding if there is a problem, but if you foist that on your employees, they'll only resent you for it. Either be willing to shell out additional money to pay for them to work odd hours or make it a policy to just handle it the next day. Remember: employees come first.

The employer's financial health can fluctuate due to either external or internal forces, the global or local economy's strength, and/or changes in laws. Businesses can cut costs by canceling projects, but since labor is a big expense, staffing cuts, a.k.a. layoffs, are used in computer companies during tough economic times. Once in my experience, rumors flew about a pending layoff, and I had to select someone to lay off. Names on the layoff list are secret and only my manager and I knew the name.

The person I put on the list had no idea his name was on the list, but he came to my office after work and begged me to tell him if his name was on the list. I told him I couldn't tell him. The next day, layoffs occurred across the entire company starting at 7 am. I called him into my office when he walked into the building and gave him what I expected was going to devastate him, but instead, he had a great big smile on his face, and couldn't resist telling me why. He had already accepted a job at another company in town for a better opportunity and showed me the envelope with his resignation letter. He was going to resign even if he wasn't laid off. That one worked out well for him and me.

During a two-year-long economic slowdown, my company reduced the amount of money available to each team for raises the first year and canceled raises the second year. I was honest with my team and told them I didn't expect to be able to reward extra effort, and I wasn't going to ask anyone to sacrifice to work hard if the raises were going to be small or none.

My manager offered me a promotion and a big raise. I turned it down because I told him there was no way I could take a raise when I couldn't give my team raises. He was shocked that anyone would turn down a promotion. I told him when the raises came back, I would be asking for that promotion, and I did, and he did. I earned a lot of respect from my team.

CHAPTER THIRTEEN
COMMUNICATIONS

HAVE YOU EVER WORKED AT A COMPANY WHOSE communication was so poor that you didn't know who to contact if there was a problem? Or have you worked at a business where staffing meetings and miscommunications happen nearly every day? If you have experienced either of those, you're not alone.

Communication is one of the most important aspects of any company, but it's also one of the most overlooked. Even if your company has its procedures and policies down pat, things can still go to pieces if you don't know who to talk to or when to talk to them. You'll also end up in an endless loop of blame when things go wrong. I have worked with some of the best and worst communicators in the industry. The best communicators know how to give credit, contact the right people when there's a problem, overcome insecurities about upper management or frontline employees, and keep an open dialogue even when it's hard. On the other hand, the worst communicators stop progress in its tracks and leave both employees and customers angry.

If you haven't already figured out communications in your company, it's about time you did. More and more people are looking for remote work, and if you don't have the right communications, your company can't survive. Communication should be your first priority. Listening is an important part of communication also. I always try to let people complete their thoughts without interruption and expect the same from my audience.

But what's the best method? Well, based on what I've seen, I can tell you from my perspective what works and what doesn't.

One thing I have consistently applied when communicating, especially in technical reports or presentations is to use the effective report writing style, simply:

1. Explain the information I am going to tell you.
2. Tell you the detailed information.
3. Summarize the information I just told you.

The very first written trip report I gave Susie B. at the hotline was rejected because it did not use this writing style and it stuck with me[1]. My presentations and reports have been consistently effective ever since.

EFFECTIVE MEETING MANAGEMENT

I think most leaders believe that a lot of meetings are absolutely necessary to complete projects, which is why they cram as many of them as they can into each week. I do agree that meetings are helpful for teams to grow and to learn from each other, but packing your days with long meetings isn't helpful for anyone. In fact, it can be pretty distracting.

There are ways to make your meetings more effective without wasting the time of your employees while still benefiting from those meetings. It all comes down to effective meeting management.

---

1. For more information, look up "writing effective reports."

Meeting Punctuality

Starting meetings late is an epidemic. Both leaders and employees are guilty of this, and it can ruin everyone's day. Meetings that don't start on time show that your team isn't working cohesively. Communication suffers when team members are late because not all the information necessary is brought to the table.

Even if your customers never realize your lack of meeting punctuality, your employees will, and it's frankly insulting. It seems like leaders don't respect the time of those working under them, and it's frustrating. If you're not careful, it can lead to higher turnover rates.

Punctuality is a very important company value. Make it a priority and expectation for your employees and customers. Starting meetings late makes them run long, and you're ultimately wasting valuable time you could be spending on projects. Late meetings also often cause a cascading effect that makes the rest of your day shift to accommodate the difference in times. If you're not careful, you could disrupt an entire day's schedule.

I realize that sometimes it's hard to make sure everyone shows up to your meetings. But people are more motivated when you prioritize punctuality and respect time management within the team meetings. The more consistent you are in your business, the more efficient you can be and the happier your employees will be. Even if you have information that goes far past your scheduled end time, save it for another day. On that same note, don't be afraid to end meetings early so everyone can get back to work.

Participation and Contribution

Your communication efficiency is only as good as your employees and leaders make it. So, if your employees feel like they can't or don't want to speak, you're missing out on some of the best information you could get from insiders in your company. Encourage everyone to discuss the status of current projects and any ideas that they have to make things better. Allow everyone to list any resources needed to close open issues, and do your best to ensure that those resources are given.

Encourage your employees to have brainstorming sessions and role-playing scenarios and break teams up into smaller groups to discuss any ideas. Make sure all your meetings are high energy, so people feel inspired to participate. You can include methods like rotating meeting roles by having different members lead different portions of the agenda and distributing responsibility. Make your employees feel like they are invested in the meeting's outcomes.

Another way to manage meetings is to bring in guests. But remember that it makes your company look bad if you don't treat guests well, which is usually enough motivation for both leaders and employees. Encourage your team to suggest people who can come in and share ideas. It will inspire your employees to participate in the selection of the next visitor.

I prefer to announce when the next agenda topic pertains directly to a member of the audience by saying his or her name, especially if the person is working from home or remotely. But I see it in person meetings because some attendees have their noses buried in their phones or laptops. Some-times an attendee is distracted by important chats from co-workers and is not paying attention.

I also like to address each person by their last name, such as Mr. Choate.

COLLABORATIVE COMMUNICATION ENVIRONMENTS

It's important to foster a collaborative environment that encourages your employees to continually learn. One of the biggest problems that I've seen in my career is that employees who don't feel like they are challenged enough tend to leave. On that same note, employees who feel like their employers aren't using them to their best abilities are wasting their talent.

I inherited a sharp Ph.D. design engineer on my team after he had completed a significant design milestone. I gave him ordinary assignments, and one day he asked for a meeting and told me he didn't feel challenged. The timing was perfect as I had been spending time researching how to automate some microprocessor performance analysis utilizing advanced debug features in our 7th and 8th generation CPUs. I painted the big picture and the enormous benefits it could have for our team productivity, and it could supercharge our race to outperform the competition on industry benchmarks. His eyes lit up and was dedicated to the project for years. It was a huge success and we both felt very proud to be granted a US Patent 6658557.

Establishing a collaborative communication environment means always talking to each other. Some companies invest in communication software while others like the old-fashioned go-up-to-coworkers-and-talk-to-them approach. I'm not saying one is better than the other. Find out which works best for you and your team. No matter which style you choose, you should always talk to someone.

I like project-specific online status collaboration, especially when I am keeping a close eye on the specific project. But it's easy for electronic notifications of status changes to be overlooked when you are flooded with notifications. One time management technique I used when my inbox was flooded was to add a reminder to an important notification. In case I don't have time to study immediately, I won't forget to get back to it.

I was usually very good at multi-tasking, but as I aged, the energy needed to multi-task diminished.

Team Learning

Teams learn best when they work together. Pick one or two

people a week to describe what they learned or how they solved problems. Have employees create short presentations and share their innovative ideas. Remember, it's all about the exchanging of ideas, so this doesn't have to be an extremely stressful project. Adding it to your routine can be a way to eliminate some of the stress that comes from giving presentations. If you include this in part of your weekly routine, Your employees will be more likely to open up.

In the software industry, it's common for introverted people to work on the same team. If you *do* have a lot of people on your team who are introverts, try pairing them with more outgoing people occasionally to mix things up. This strategy doesn't always work, so be especially mindful of your employees so they don't feel too miserable. But, encouraging your employees to get into slightly uncomfortable situations can help them learn to overcome insecurities in discussing problems. It's a great way to promote team growth.

Encourage your team to continually learn. If you have it in the budget, pay employees to get outside education to improve themselves. You want your company and especially your team to be seen as the hub for employee curiosity and engagement.

One day, Gary A., a young man who worked in the in-house IT department as a technician, made an appointment to get my advice on changing jobs and how to be a successful supervisor or manager. I always jokingly referred to him as our "cable monkey." He had an outgoing personality, a friendly smile, was a particularly good verbal & non-verbal communicator, and was exceptionally enthusiastic about doing a good job.

I remember advising Gary about the language of management —budgeting for success and managing costs and expenses.

The next thing I knew, Gary was moving up the management ladder at rocket speed because 1) he was always impeccably well-dressed and well-spoken, 2) he created impressive presentations about saving money in manufacturing operations, and 3) he accepted challenging projects that no one else wanted to do.

He ardently completed training classes offered by both the company and outside firms to gain manager skill knowledge and put them to effective use. He later helped build, expand, and manage the R&D department of multiple overseas systems engineering teams. He continued to vigorously educate himself and his teams. Gary was very highly regarded by other managers within the organization

Keep a running board that shows innovations, tools, and methodologies for professional growth and company development. Share those ideas with the team often. Make it a game to see what you can add to the innovations list and see if you can incorporate some of that technology or outside techniques to make your team run better.

One of our system debug tools was a JTAG wiggler box developed for internal use that was also available for advanced customers with reduced features to help them develop their own custom motherboard designs. The connection to the box was a cable connector on the top layer of the motherboard, but customers complained it required too much board space for the connector and related components. Also, the host laptop computer ran the tool software connected with a cable directly, limiting the distance between the system under test (SUT) and the host laptop.

This one little detail in the overall system design threatened a reduction in sales of our most advanced and competitive microprocessors.

Donald C, one of my debug engineers, took the initiative and made it his mission to miniaturize the connection and include a host ethernet connection. This was an incredibly challenging project; the R&D expense was underfunded but Donald never gave up. The eventual benefits of Donald's proposed innovative project proved too enormous to ignore. Resources were assigned, new budgets were created, and it became the new standard used for years on many generations of CPUs.

Initially, the miniature flat ribbon cable used for the board connection was unshielded leading to both data transfer speed limitations due to signal loss and crosstalk. Another issue was seen when static from the plastic wheels of office chairs discharged. The cable acted like an antenna, causing the SUT to malfunction. I requested the team to design a custom miniature shielded cable to solve that problem. Each wire in the new flat ribbon cable was a miniature shielded coax.

Respectful and Transparent Language

If you're doing it right, your team should feel so open that anybody can express their thoughts on solutions and problems. So, if you feel like your employees can't honestly talk to you and don't feel safe about expressing their concerns, it's time to provide some training on how to effectively communicate. This is a great tool for both leaders and employees. Activities that promote active listening, assertiveness, and empathy help employees address issues head-on.

No matter what you do, you'll run into people who don't want to share what they're thinking. For those employees who feel like their emotions are bottled up, they may express themselves in passive-aggressive language. Know the signs of passive aggressiveness and have tools for alleviating tensions. If you hear sarcasm, indirect resistance, or subtle sabotage within your team, call it out immediately. It's best to cut off passive-aggressive behavior openly to make sure that it doesn't have any negative impacts on your team. Instead, focus on promoting positivity in language.

In the same vein, be very transparent in your communication. Avoid misunderstandings that can cause stress on your team. Be specific about what you want from everyone, and let anyone ask questions if they don't understand what is required. Regularly check in with your employees on a one-to-one basis so they don't feel pressure in a group setting.

Once tasks are complete, give team members feedback on what was done correctly and what needs improvement. This is a common technique for new hires, but it's also very useful for people who have been there a while. Even the best communicators have misunderstandings every once in a while, so, as a leader, when you acknowledge that you might have your own limitations, your employees will be much more likely to express their feelings.

Recognize any valuable input that participants make. Sometimes employees feel like they can't express what they're thinking because they're worried about how it will be seen. Quieter employees are usually the most difficult to get out of their shells, but if they feel like they have a friendly environment that supports them, they can offer some of the best suggestions. Make sure that you're boosting individual confidence and recognizing all the contributions people make to a project's success.

But, like with all workplaces, some people try to dominate the discussion. A lot of times these dominant individuals can overshadow quieter participants. If you want quieter employees to feel comfortable enough to share, set ground rules before every meeting to make sure that everyone has an equal speaking time. Use your skills as a leader to steer conversations to the strengths of your employees. If there are a lot of interruptions, remind everyone that there are sharing rules, and everyone should be respectful of new speakers.

CONTRIBUTION RECOGNITION AND REWARDS

Getting attention is vital to human development. Everyone from young children to people well over a century old need to feel a connection with somebody to succeed. We all need to be recognized at some point, and recognition at work can be spare. When was the last time you were recognized for your work?

Sometimes, a person is so eager for a big pat on the back of achievement that they could prematurely announce a breakthrough. It's embarrassing to announce a new solution to a tough, highly visible problem but later discover a mistake was made and the issue you were investigating was not resolved—it's like peeling an onion: the deeper you go the stinkier it gets. Sometimes, the change needed to resolve one problem creates another new problem or masks a different problem.

When someone on my team comes to me with an unbelievable breakthrough seeking praise and recognition, I can see the disappointment on their faces when I ask how confident they are of the findings. If they've done due diligence, I'll ask them to prove it or insist on seeing the results for myself just to make sure the unbelievable feat was indeed real and reliable.

Achievement Celebration

Once, when my team was testing the first processor to achieve 1GHz operating speed with new metal interconnects using copper instead of tungsten, everything went well except when a certain brand of third-party joystick failed to be detected. This was a show-stopper type of problem found late in the pre-production readiness phase.

The engineer debugging the issue was making no progress in debugging the cause of the issue, so I ordered him to regress the problem by reducing the CPU speed from 1GHz to 900MHz. Lo and behold, the joystick initialized correctly and worked flawlessly.

I instructed him to write a standalone diagnostic script that replicated the joystick detection sequence to eliminate everything else from the system. I also asked him to instrument the code to output the status port data to a debug test port so we could see the timing and data of the joystick status port reads with a logic analyzer trace.

Through experimentation, he discovered the status port was ultra-sensitive to the rate of status port reads. Because the CPU executed at higher speeds, it was reading the port at a higher rate than expected by the joystick hardware, causing it to fail. The finding eradicated the last gate to starting production.

The reward was shared by the entire team; for getting the new landmark processor ready to ship, we created a beautiful team T-shirt with "1GHz" emblazoned with copper colored lettering and gave it to everyone. We also gave a personalized certificate of appreciation to the engineer at the weekly team meeting. The T-shirt was eye-catching and appreciated by everyone.

As you might have picked up from the rest of the chapter, communication is much more than just avoiding misunderstandings. It's about building confidence in your team and encouraging employees to relax and enjoy their work. A lot of that comes from the open celebration of outstanding achievements. Publicly praise team members periodically. You might want to consider giving formal awards or a personalized speech. The goal is to make sure that employees want to strive for excellence, but that shouldn't be your first instinct. If your words are truly heartfelt, you'll inspire your entire team.

If you're doing it right, you'll create a trickle-down effect. Essentially, you're creating an example of valuing the contributions of your team members. The faster you can foster appreciation between leaders and employees, the more likely coworkers are to get along with each other. You could encourage coworkers to show more appreciation by creating a wall of fame that anyone can add to which will create a more supportive and motivating workplace.

TEAM BONDING

Have you ever worked in a place where people simply didn't want to talk to each other? There are too many places out there that focus more on efficiency and production than they do on making sure that their employees are happy. To me, that just makes working there a nightmare. Leaders should want to boost their teams' morale and mood.

Outside of just making your workplace an area where people are excited to work together, think about how you can make your team a more positive place. Share stories in the break room that have nothing to do with work. Support each other in both professional and personal achievements. The more you do things for people when you "don't have to," the closer your team will feel.

It's the small things that make a big difference, like offering appreciation and even the occasional gift certificate. I really like to bring treats to my regular team meetings. My treat of choice was always the world-famous Round Rock donuts. You can't go wrong when your team is sharing fried dough.

Impact and Value Highlights

Last, make your communication stand out and last the test of time. Writing down what team members have achieved not only improves morale in your team but can give your company a good reputation. Keep track of key metrics, outcomes, and testimonials from people who have seen positive results because of other team members or customers. By keeping a paper trail, you can connect the dots when things go right and reward the right person.

Of course, this leads directly to helping your employees get motivated by showing concrete evidence of their success. A generalized "good job" doesn't cut it. Most employees who feel like they're just getting recognition as part of a participation program will feel even worse than they would if they hadn't gotten any praise at all. But attaching metrics that show how employees work with the company goals can help you create a continuous cycle of improvement and motivation in your employees.

On that same note, make the performance tracking transparent. Allow achievements to be shared with the team, and make coworkers accountable for each other. There's no shame in asking your employees how their contributions fit into the company's larger picture. It's a great way to build trust and help everyone celebrate successes collectively.

During the pre-production testing phase of the first 64-bit x86 processor, I was flooded with urgent requests for the status of the backlog of issues. The project was a secret because we hadn't yet officially announced it. I created a template for importing, analyzing, and sorting all the issues and plotted the weekly new and closed issues by category and priority on multiple charts sorted in different ways based on how key people wanted to see the data. I published it to all the stakeholders and my team weekly. The status reports became almost legendary for capturing an up-to-date snapshot of the ever-changing systems debug world.

Share the reports that you create both as individuals and as a team with upper management. As a leader, making your team as visible as possible will ensure that the right people get recognized. Your team should be at the top of your priority list, and that comes with an advanced amount of communication.

CHAPTER FOURTEEN
CONFERENCE PLANNING

Though this might be one of the shortest chapters in the book, I'm including it because conference planning is so important. After the COVID-19 pandemic, things came to a standstill in terms of in-person conferencing, which is such a shame. Now, with all the online conferencing software, it's easier to do conferencing without actually meeting in person or traveling.

But there's so much that's missing when you're not meeting people in person. You don't get a chance to sit down with some of the leaders in the industry to talk about what they have recently discovered. That also means that you don't have the chance to share your ideas in a large group setting. The verbal and nonverbal cues that you get from meeting people in person can lead to better brainstorming and collaboration between companies and departments. Giving yourself the chance to form friendships when visiting people who work in your sector is also gone in a remote setting.

Of course, because conference planning has largely become remote now, the art of creating conferences has also gone down the drain. But, if you're one of those people who really wants to start a more collaborative conference experience like I do, here are some tips to get you started.

PLANNING AND SCHEDULING

When first organizing your conference or summit, look at a realistic timeline. Starting conferencing on your own means talking with vendors and other companies to set up a conference that will benefit people nationwide, but many of the tips apply to internal confidential conferences or individual customer conferences also. That usually means that you need at least six weeks to set everything up. You'll get time to coordinate all the necessary details, which includes securing venues and booking speakers. The faster you can secure a venue and people to come to your conference and participate in it the faster you can make changes if there is some sort of disruption.

When you're setting up your conference, pay attention to a detailed timeline that includes milestones and individual company deadlines. You want to make sure that your conferences build on previous events and encourage people to participate. Set up methods to instill the importance of maintaining relationships over time.

During your process, evaluate your processes as often as possible to make sure that you're on track. Get feedback from attendees, companies, and stakeholders on who they think would be the best speakers in the industry and who would have the most offer. The more feedback you get, the more valuable your conference is to more people. It helps you with a long-term marketing strategy so you can hopefully continue your conferences year after year.

There's a lot that goes into scheduling and planning a conference, and it's no easy task. But here are some suggestions to get you started.

. . .

Inviting and Engaging Stakeholders and Speakers

CONFERENCES COST A LOT OF MONEY. THAT'S WHY YOU need the backing of several companies and stakeholders to make sure that your conference is a success. So, take some time to brainstorm which stakeholders have the most to gain from these conferences. Find which stakeholders and suppliers are interested in developing innovation and coming up with solutions to common challenges. You could mention the processes, tools, and features that are most beneficial to them.

The easiest place to find stakeholders is within your immediate organization. But, if you want to get more engagement from people nationwide, look for people who have fresh perspectives and new ideas. Engage people who will invite a diverse range of participants and broaden your scope.

Suggest collaboration with other companies that could include valuable partnerships and collaborations. It's a great opportunity to see if you're on the same page with other people in your industry. Whether your company is new or old, there are always new partnerships that can really add to what you offer.

Your goal is to encourage guests to want to participate, which usually means offering workshops, panel discussions, and breakout sessions. So, start thinking now about who most people would want to engage with in informal discussions, including networking breaks and social events. If you truly value what some of these stakeholders can offer in terms of driving participation, let them know! Everyone likes to hear that what they contribute is not only informative but also inspiring and impactful.

Working with Speakers

YOU SHOULD HAVE A LIST OF SPEAKERS CONFIRMED NO less than four months before your conference and summit. They are the driving factor behind attendance at your summit; work with them to find out what they think is most important in engineering. Work with the speaker to create a guide that shows the expectations, presentation guidelines, and technical requirements that speakers need to be the most effective in delivering their speeches and workshops. Confirm with them early to make sure that there aren't any last-minute changes.

Ask speakers if they have any colleagues or know thought leaders that they think would be an asset to your conference. Coordinate with speakers on how specific you want your conference to be, and encourage them to come up with suggestions to make it more specific for attendees. Your topic can go as broad as you want it to, but remember that your goal is to make your conference as cohesive as possible.

Finalizing Agendas

CREATE A WELL-STRUCTURED OUTLINE OF THE MAIN topics and themes you want to cover in your summit. I always found that debugging summits were some of the most interesting, and I could tell which would be most beneficial to me and my team by looking at the speakers and workshop leaders. I have captured innovative debug technology presented by others during the summits and adapted it to new generations of microprocessors. So, confirm early what the topics of keynote speeches, panel discussions, workshops, and breakout sessions will be so you can encourage as many people to participate as possible.

My debugging summit theme was the dream of developing self-healing computers. It was very inspirational. Computer hardware glitches do occur, and they should be automatically detected and corrected. An example of that is laptops during airplane travel. Gamma rays at high altitudes can cause computing upsets. If they can be properly detected and corrected on the fly without increasing the cost of laptops, it is a win-win. Modern DDR5 memory devices include error check and scrubbing features for this very reason.

As soon as you have an outline draft, make sure that you don't have any potential conflicts or gaps and that there is enough time for each speaker in each session. Include time for setup, transitions, and informal meetings and breaks for networking, refreshments, And conversation.

Once you've completed the agenda, get feedback from your stakeholders and speakers to refine the agenda even more. Remember, you're looking to make your conference as accessible to everyone in the industry as possible, which means that outside perspectives are often your best secret weapon. Ask for any feedback on how you can adjust things to make your conference as engaging as possible.

As soon as you're done, put the final agenda on your website and encourage people to participate in spreading the information. Include highlights and the conference's main agenda in your outline, and encourage companies to send employees to get additional information and training. To make it even more engaging, create a mobile-friendly version of the agenda that is easy to access before and during your conference. It's a great way to make sure that your participants know of any last-minute changes or additions to the outline.

Promoting the Event

KEEP IN MIND THAT ONE OF THE MOST IMPORTANT ways to make your conference successful is to promote it properly. Create a marketing plan that includes your target audience, your key messaging, and any promotional channels that would be beneficial to promoting your event. Create digital marketing strategies such as e-mail campaigns, social media, and content marketing which can reach a broader audience than simply from your website. Think of this as a great opportunity to network.

Use partnerships and collaborations with your speakers and your stakeholders to get the word out. Remember that your conference is all about the sharing of ideas, so you can promote your conference by letting people know that your goal is to promote innovation. People who follow your stakeholders and speakers will want to hear what new things are out there.

Consider offering incentives for signing up, like early bird discounts, group rates, or referral bonuses that companies can use to increase registrations for your event. Usually, you can find influencers or other leaders in the industry that can promote your conference. Those personal testimonials and endorsements can really add to your conference's credibility, and it's a great way to attract more people.

CONDUCTING SUMMITS

When the day of the event arrives, you're in for even more work. If you want to reengage and encourage people to start coming to summits in person again, you'll need to have a bit of a spectacle. That all comes down to making sure that everything goes off without a hitch. All your attendees should already know everything that's going to happen in your conference before they arrive, and you should try to exceed those expectations.

Curating Content and Speakers

ONCE YOU HAVE EVERYONE ALREADY AT YOUR conference, make finding workshops and attending lectures easy. Set up your venue with references to themes and topics so it's easier to navigate. Give each participant a hard copy of a schedule of your conferences so they can know the itinerary.

Encourage your speakers and workshop curators to have literature on hand that they can hand out to the participants. This is a great opportunity for anyone who is marketing a book or selling courses to advertise what they do. Give your participants access to as much information as they can get on your speakers.

Fostering Networking Opportunities

NETWORKING IS LIKELY ONE OF THE BIGGEST DRAWS TO your conference. Companies want to know about new talent and technology, and participants want to learn new things and engage in brainstorming and discussion. So, to make sure that everyone can network as much as they'd like, set aside a conference room or buffet line that can serve as the room for marketing professionals.

You can also set up technology stations or discussion hubs that make it easier for people interested in the same subjects to congregate. Thinking of it as setting up structured activities that work as speed networking sessions that also allow people to gain great friendships.

Consider helping participants network more effectively by giving them networking booklets or even just sheets of paper where they can write down the profiles of their favorite speakers, meetings that they want to have with other professionals, and notes during discussions. At the end of your conference, everyone should feel like they've made new friends.

Offering Hands-On Learning Experiences

IF YOU CAN, SET UP VERY HANDS-ON WORKSHOPS OR live demonstrations. Any new skills or knowledge that offers immediate applicability is very enticing. Attendees can share what they learn with their companies or come up with their own innovations. It's a great chance to get practical experience with the latest tools and technology under the guidance of someone who works with these tools daily.

Consider offering a variety of skill levels that make it easier for people who are already familiar with those tools to gain new knowledge. Both beginners and advanced developers should have access to learning new things. It might be a good opportunity to give more advanced developers the chance to talk with workshop and summit leaders during these hands-on experiences.

ENGAGING FEEDBACK

Maybe the most fun part of the summit is finding out what people think about it. It's a great way to make sure that you are continuously improving the process, and it makes it easier for other people who want to do their own conferences to set up something successful.

This kind of transparency builds trust and encourages sponsors, stakeholders, and speakers to come back. If you're organized enough, you can continually update your feedback strategies to make sure that you are as responsive as possible to attendees' needs and expectations. The more time you spend on making sure you catch mistakes that were made in previous summits, the more likely you are to have successful conferences in the future.

Capturing Comprehensive Notes and Summaries

BEFORE YOUR ATTENDEES LEAVE THE CONFERENCE, make sure that you get as many notes as possible about the success of your conference. Ask people for feedback on what was done well and what wasn't, and save the results in a place that is accessible to many people. Assign note takers to use recording devices during sessions to make sure that there was no critical information missed. If you're creating a national conference, it can seem overwhelming to get all the notes you need, so make sure you get back up.

When creating your notes, highlight key points and major takeaways that participants got from their sessions. Find out if they liked the sessions and what they would want for future conferences. Set up a way for them to continually engage you online so that they can produce their own strategies. That's a very effective way of making sure that you are networking effectively and maintaining a good collaboration with other companies.

Use social media to get feedback on the experiences of participants. You can get immediate feedback and highlight issues that need attention in the future. If you go into social media with a multi-channel approach, you can reach a wide variety of people from your audience. Try to get as many perspectives as possible so you can make as many positive changes as you can. Internal and/or single-customer conferences just need to capture private feedback and action items, then follow up with progress on the action items.

When you're done, distribute the summaries to participants as part of a newsletter, and add the notes you received to your website in PDF digital format. Give them the option to save the information long-term.

Analyzing and Acting on Feedback

IDENTIFY ANY KEY PATTERNS THAT SHOW UP WHEN YOU do get your feedback. Most of the time, people have roughly the same complaints and positive feedback. You're looking for widespread thoughts from your attendees. It can seem like a lot to manually sort the feedback, but you can always get help or use qualitative data analysis software to make it easier on you.

Once you've gotten a handle on what most people think, create a report that highlights the most common feedback. Share that feedback on social media and your website to show that you are looking to be as transparent as possible. Also, the more feedback you include, the more people will feel like their opinions are heard, which is important to make sure they come back at the next summit. Another great strategy for using a summary of the feedback is sharing it on social media, which can be displayed as recommendations for your company.

EPILOGUE

I turned down an opportunity to go to Annapolis Naval Academy for officer training in high school and deliberately failed the final panel interview as a top three qualifier round of competition to win a scholarship to a diesel mechanic school because I wanted to work on computers.

    I worked at John Mizell Texaco car wash and gas station in my hometown of San Angelo, Texas. I made friends with one of my customers, a manager at General Telephone (GTE). I asked him his opinion of the best electronics school. He told me it was the Electronics Institute of Technology at Texas A&M. I had a brochure for that school. I had been enrolled previously at DeVry Institute in Dallas but made a trip up there with my father and frankly was not impressed, so I forfeited my deposit because I thought it wasn't the school I wanted to attend. I found the brochure for the school at Texas A&M and called them the next Friday. They said classes start Monday and encouraged me to "come on down." So, I quit my job, packed my bags, and called my cousin, Annette, who managed an apartment complex, and she let me stay in her spare room.

    There were 60 students at the beginning, and we graduated

with 20. I took my final exam in the first semester with a slide rule because electronic calculators were too expensive. My family was dirt poor. I bought a cheap Commodore Scientific calculator for my second semester. I finished in the top three of the class. I had four job offers before graduation. One employer apologized for giving us the engineering test given to four-year BSEE graduates instead of the Electronic Engineering Technician test, I finished first and scored highest in the class because our classes were taught by the same professors as the four-year BSEE class, but our classes were based on the newest textbooks prior to approval by the State Board of Education required for the four-year program. Later, the pre-employment tests were determined to discriminate against low-income job applicants and tests were eliminated. I chose Austin aka Silicon Hills because it was a great place to live.

I started my journey at Texas A&M, studying applied physics, math, and electronics theory. Once out of college, I was fortunate to start work at the 990 Unit Test along with 3 other Texas A&M classmates in February 1976. It's where I got the opportunity to learn debugging from "Hotdog." The way he explained data architecture and how to use it to debug computers was one of the most significant schoolings that influenced my career, alongside my education. Because our CPU in 1976 was constructed using four discrete 4-bit slice ALUs (Arithmetic Logic Units) with the carry and borrow signals cascading to make a 16-bit processor using 256-deep PROMs (that carried the microcode), internal operations visibility was fundamental. I was curious how everything worked. And it was right there in front of me. Every microstep of the microcode for a macro-operation was observable. I learned how to connect a logic analyzer, step through each of the instructions, and watch how each of the instructions worked. The value of visibility was permanently impressed upon me.

I was destined to spend the next 47 years focusing on debugging and testing and failure analysis, culminating in pioneering changes that had an immense impact on the industry.

THE DEBUGGING JOURNEY

When power was applied to computers in 1976, they initially stopped after a system reset state, waiting for someone to give them a starting address for the first instruction. They did not even have a power-on self-testing routine that all modern computers now use.

Typically, the user pressed soft, calculator-style buttons on the front panel: HLT (halt), RST (reset), next pressing a series of up to 16 buttons representing a 16-bit binary value 0 through 65,535 that toggled on red LEDs (Light Emitting diodes) for a starting address, and finally pressed the LOAD and RUN buttons, which started execution. A LOAD setting of 80 hex was reserved for a digital cassette tape device, 82 for a punched card reader, and 84 for paper tape. The load device then read the media and converts it to digital bytes. The interface card then stored the data in memory. The front panel was used again to start the new loader, which stored a main program from disk, 9-track tape, or punched cards into memory.

As the computer started running, by default the LEDs would periodically flash progress codes, but the information was displayed in binary, which we mentally converted to hexadecimal to relate to its encoded meaning. The progress code type was selectable using miniature toggle switches on the main board. For debug, we could select error codes. If the last instruction prior to a timer-tick interrupt was selected, we could tell what it was doing before it crashed, and if the LEDs stopped flashing, we could tell the system was locked up or had crashed.

Everyone had boxes of punched cards for their favorite test programs, and every once in a while, I found a software bug in the program by decoding the machine codes. I learned how to hack the program in memory using the front panel, but I sometimes needed to insert instructions. It was easier to take the punched card to a machine that read it and edited the codes, print a new card, and insert it in the deck. There were usually a few NOPs in the code that could be re-defined as active instructions. If the modification worked, I filed a bug report and got the test owner to update the source code. I memorized every instruction and could instantly decode the hex memory into the instructions they represented. I became the best debugger on the team. I was usually the person who trained new members of the test team on debugging and testing.

The front panel was controlled by a simple state machine on the System Memory Interface (SMI) board. It used scan codes to determine which button was pressed. Previous computers used mechanical toggle switches, so this was a big improvement. The red LEDs were not controlled by the buttons, they were programmed by the state machine programmed to display selected information as buttons were pressed. There was also a HALT button and a Single-step button to step through processor instructions one at a time. There were also buttons to display or change selected general-purpose internal registers.

When a new product came out, called the Advanced Microprocessor Programming Lab (AMPL), I was chosen to bring up, develop, write, and execute the test plan. It was designed by Barry P. and was the industry's first In-Circuit Emulator (ICE) for the first 16-bit processor integrated circuit. It was basically a logic analyzer on steroids. It was a debug tool for microprocessors. It could log, Start/Stop, and control the actions of the microprocessor. It had its own programming language with macros written in assembly language, or machine instructions. But it also had a higher-level language like PASCAL and BASIC with IF-THEN_ELSE, CASE, and LOOP constructs. I became an expert on the ICE. I learned a lot about microprocessor design, and it stuck with me. I gave many suggestions for improvements back to the design team.

After spending 4 years at the help desk, I walked into Albert Johnson's office after solving several big customer problems in the field for him and offered to work for him. He put me in charge of the Field Communications team where my team, Dale R., Earl R., and Cesar reviewed all the changes to components from all sources, and revisions on boards or major subsystems that had an impact of any kind on our field service operations or inventories. Beth and Linda typed the documents on a typewriter, got signature approvals, and sent them to a print shop to snail-mail them to all our field offices around the world. Sometimes it was urgent to notify the field, and we faxed urgent notices. Many years later we just emailed the electronic documents to the offices.

I also inherited the field support engineer hotline team since I was already directing much of their technical work anyway. Sometimes, if nobody else could solve a problem, I would travel to the customer site to help analyze and solve the problem. I got such a good reputation that they took away my manager title and focused my attention on solving problems, field quality, and reliability.

One such instance involved a new disk drive interface called SCSI (pronounced "scuzzy", Small Computer Systems Interface). I had previously worked with the designer of the interface and knew him well. Our system could support up to four SCSI drives on one cable, but if one of them failed, it was not easy to determine which one caused the problem because all four drives shared the same interface. I designed an adapter that fit on the cable that latched the SCSI ID of the last drive to get a command, and usually, the one that failed was the last accessed.

I also pioneered disk data recovery and trained the field personnel on how to recover customer-lost data, which we turned into a profitable service. I became so well-known and successful in the computing industry that I taught courses on disk and tape controllers in Germany, France, and Singapore.

Later in my career—after 1994—my experience naturally led me to advanced microprocessors.

I became the manager of the system debug team, grossing a $2M capital budget just for logic analyzers. When a new logic analyzer was developed, their companies contacted me in the hopes that I'd be the first person to use a prototype. I'd give feedback for improvements and point out what I liked and disliked. I got Tektronix to add network capability to their machines, including approximately 8 improvements added to the TLA series of logic analyzers[1].

When my company licensed the DEC Alpha bus for our main control interface, there was no logic analyzer capability due to a variety of factors, such as encoded commands and responses. So, an internal team and I developed our own bus analyzer with multiple Mictor™ connectors to connect to a TLA (Tektronix Logic Analyzer). Since that team had also developed the Northbridge FPGA, it was not terribly difficult to change it into a logic analyzer.

The main principle of failure analysis is visibility into what the system is doing. Even if it was impossible to see exactly what the CPU was doing, I could infer the internal state indirectly by analyzing the messages that appeared on the main control bus and comparing a passing case to a failing case.

Later, Samsung bought the DEC Alpha design, and I just happened to have a job interview with one of their design managers. The subject of the logic analyzer for the DEC Alpha bus came up. He said no one could figure out how to do it, and I told him how *we* did it. He offered me a job in California, but I turned it down. I spent 9-months on a temporary assignment in Silicon Valley previously and knew the cost of living was way too high for my family.

---

1. Logic analyzers were very expensive and had limitations, especially as the bus speeds increased over 100 MHz

I was instrumental in the development of several advanced built-in tracing features in our new processors that significantly increased the efficiency of the debug processes for just about any component on the system. It allowed us to obtain the information we usually obtained from logic analyzers without inserting a probing card into the machine. State-of-the-art logic analyzers, a.k.a. protocol analyzers, used mid-bus probing techniques to capture and analyze the signals, but anytime a probe connected, it interfered with the quality of the electrical signal. Built-in tracing features eliminated the need for mid-bus probing on certain high-speed interfaces.

THE "CPU WHISPERER"

After analyzing a failure, my team recommended solutions to the appropriate design team. I wasn't responsible for implementing them because the design team would often have a better solution. I enjoyed supervising the day-to-day debugging of every issue in our lab. I also kept a watchful eye on all the testing in other teams looking for other types of failure that could be caused by the same thing we were investigating. If we could correlate different test failures to the same thing, we could increase the closure rate. We always gave priority to issues that looked like a hardware design problem.

I also excelled at analyzing certain types of microprocessor manufacturing defects. I pioneered the use of a technique we called socket-level-lockstep and filed five patents. Only three were issued. We called the main system board "SHERLOCK" and one of the smaller boards "WATSON," named after the great fictional detective and his partner. We developed a crack team of engineers including key members like Steve, Marco, Michael, Mark, Heather, Srivini, and Hooi-min. One of the engineers on the project, Arthur R., gave me the nickname "CPU Whisperer."

I learned there is a logical explanation for everything, but the proof may be elusive. There really *is* a logical explanation for everything, but not all explanations are logical.

"WHO ARE YOU?"

The corporation I worked with for many years divested itself of many of its businesses in 1992, deciding the land my division used was more valuable than the operations, so they sold us. Only about 400 of the 4000 employees were offered jobs in the transfer. I had to find something else to do.

I immediately started a business out of my house and eventually opened a store on the main street of my suburb town called Mike Choate Gadget Repair and Custom Design. I designed custom cables for things like surveying equipment and timers for forensic cadaver research for the Texas Department of Safety and custom 386 computers for businesses. A young man named Michael Dell made custom computers in his dorm room in 1984 and became very successful. If he could do it, why couldn't I?

I eventually applied for a job advertised in the local printed newspaper by a contracting agency called Aerotech. 3 months later, in August 1994, I got a call for an interview for an electronic technician contingent-worker position. My phone interview with the systems engineering department manager David B resulted in a personal interview. This three-initial company was based in Silicon Valley but had a major design center here in Silicon Hills. I interviewed and got the impression they wanted to hire me starting the next Monday.

I showed up the next Monday for the job, and the hiring manager, a Swede named Hans, said "We didn't hire you, but while you are here, we can put you to work."

They gave me a contingent-worker badge and assigned me the task of analyzing a failure that only occurred when OS software starting with the letter "W" was launched in paging mode at high temperature and high speed, 80 MHz. I used a thermal head connected to a 486 processor on an interposer with a Tektronix DAS 9200 analyzer and a 486 protocol analysis package to capture the bus traces leading to the failure and compared them to a correlated passing trace at a lower temperature. I pinpointed the differences and determined the cause of the malfunction in 2 weeks of careful analysis.

My traces were converted into an ATE tester pattern by a test engineer named Curtis G. It was the first time a system failure correlated to an ATE tester pattern. A design engineer named Dave K. used micro-probing to isolate the test failure to a circuit malfunction caused by a timing speed path in the unified L1 Translation Lookaside Buffer (TLB) cache. (Early 486 CPUs used a common cache bank for both instruction (ICache) and data (DCache) operations. Modern computers have independent cache banks for ICache and DCache. Back then, the silicon die was attached to the package using a wire-bonding attachment technique. He corrected the problem in the metal layers and my company led the industry for 9 months with high-volume production. We made more profit during those 9 months than the company had lost in their entire 25-year history. I didn't get to enjoy the profit-sharing bonus because the regulated employment date was Jan 1, they didn't convert me to a regular employee until Jan 3, 1995.

I had no shortage of work. We had a new chip to compete with our competitor's latest 5th generation x86 microprocessor. We called it the Krypton project because the media referred to our competitor as the "Superman" of the industry—indestructible.

One of the most memorable issues I analyzed was a serial mouse failure running the OS. The mouse driver had a timing loop in it, and the x86 instruction in our advanced CPU executed the timing loop 6 times faster than the competitor processor. I recommended we slow down the instruction to make it work. I found that a different competitor had a microcode patch to slow their timing loop down. Our brilliant design team said "no" because it was a software problem, not a hardware problem, and there was no way they were going to slow down their design for a software problem. I did more research and found a software setting that changed the mouse driver to an interrupt-driven timing loop and solved the problem. This was prior to the introduction of USB or Bluetooth Mice.

Shortly thereafter, I was tasked with analyzing the low performance of several benchmarks. I collected DAS 9200 traces and concluded that too many redundant memory accesses occurred, which slowed down the execution of the benchmark. The microprocessor chief architect, Mike J., the man who "wrote the college textbook on RISC processors" was also our company's Chief Technical Officer (CTO). Just after I converted to full-time, I had a shiny new badge and had to make a presentation to Mike J. and the top designers in the company. I made a radical recommendation for a design change that ultimately solved the performance problem. Mike J. had his own ideas for solving the performance problem and rejected my recommendation. Nobody had ever heard of my name. They looked at me like "Who are you? Where did you get your Ph.D.? How many books have you written?" I did not have an advanced degree and had authored no books on microprocessor theory, so I had no standing in the industry[2].

I applied for my PE license and passed two tests before I started this job: the Principles and Practices of Engineering test and the Fundamentals of Engineering test. I have known people with 4-year degrees who couldn't pass the tests in four attempts. They are tough tests. I earned the Professional Engineer license because of my experience and years of working with other PEs who recommended me to the state licensing board. It was

---

2. Everyone knows what an EE, BSEE, or MSEE is. I was an EET, Electronic Engineering Technician. A friend of mine who designs communication hardware and software calls himself a Comm-E (pronounced commie). I guess that makes us silicon engineers a Sil-E engineer (Silly ha-ha).

extremely rare that an applicant without a 4-year college degree would be granted a PE license, but I was granted my license just a few days later on February 4, 1995. I renewed it annually until about 2006, then I let it expire. I didn't really need it for the work I was doing. But it let me put the word "engineer" on my business card. This was important to me.

FROM START TO FINISH

Well, that covers just a fraction of my career from 1976 until about 2002, and a sliver of work I did up until 2006. I had my PE license from 1995 until about 2005 when I decided not to renew it anymore. I never really needed it to perform my work, but it gave me status and the legal ability to add the title "Engineer" to my business cards.

I apologize if I left anyone out that helped me. I didn't write this book to make it appear I was better than anyone else; I wrote it to share my unique story and hopefully some useful information. I shared the stories to make a specific point about how visibility into the internal operation is so important to understand the causes of problems to determine a solution. Keeping an open mind and trusting that there really is a logical explanation for everything is a key focus of my success.

I also wrote this book to provide a glimpse into the history of a help desk for minicomputers. Many talented people work at help desks. Some are definitely overqualified because they need a survivor job. Give people a chance to contribute at their highest level. Provide training.

I think technology should be used to improve mankind, not destroy it. If after reading this book, you decide to distrust technology, I don't blame you.

ACKNOWLEDGMENTS

Thank you to Stu Barrett for his invaluable contributions to this book. And a special thanks to Katie Barrett and Thomas Choate for their insightful advice and guidance.
Thank you all for your exceptional support.

www.ingramcontent.com/pod-product-compliance
Lightning Source LLC
Chambersburg PA
CBHW020757160426
43192CB00006B/357